EVERYDAY WISDOM

FOR LIFE

FROM THE BOOK OF PROVERBS

Cynthia Down

i

COPYRIGHT, SOURCES AND CONTRIBUTORS

SOURCES:

Unless otherwise indicated, all Scripture quotations are taken from the Holy Bible, New Living Translation, copyright © 1996, 2004, 2007, 2013 by Tyndale House Foundation. Used by permission of Tyndale House Publishers, Inc., Carol Stream, Illinois 60188. All rights reserved.

Where NASB is referenced: Scripture quotations taken from the New American Standard Bible®,Copyright © 1960, 1962, 1963, 1968, 1971, 1972, 1973, 1975, 1977, 1995 by The Lockman Foundation. Used by permission." (www.Lockman.org)

Where NIV is referenced: Bible, 1978. Edwin H. Palmer et al., *The Holy Bible, New International Version: Containing the Old Testament and the New Testament*. Grand Rapids: Zondervan, 1978. Revised in 1984 and in 2011.

Extensive use of: "BibleGateway." *.com: A Searchable Online Bible in over 100 Versions and 50 Languages.* N.p., n.d. Web.

Extensive use of: "Bible Hub: Search, Read, Study the Bible in Many Languages." *Bible Hub: Search, Read, Study the Bible in Many Languages*. Biblos.com, n.d. Web. <http://biblehub.com/>.

Merriam Webster definitions: "Discernment." *Merriam-Webster.com*. Merriam-Webster, n.d. Web. 14 Nov. 2014. <http://www.merriam-webster.com/dictionary/discernment>.

CONTRIBUTORS:

Editor: Ebook Editing Services, PO Box 39906, Los Angeles, CA 90039, http://www.ebookeditingservices.com/

Cover Design: Dave Down, mediaLEGENDS.com

Dedicated to my mom, Kathy Baker. I love you and miss you. I know you would be proud.

Special and loving thanks to my wonderful husband, David Down. I couldn't have done this without you! You're my technical guru and marketing genius. I love and adore you forever.

For the glory of God

TABLE OF CONTENTS

INTRODUCTION

Do you crave straightforward and fulfilling guidance for everyday life issues?

Do you find advice offered in the world today leaves you feeling dissatisfied and empty…unchanged?

Do you long for a refreshing change of perspective and meaningful insight into daily living?

You desire wisdom!

You have come to the right place. The satisfaction you seek comes from the ancient wisdom of Proverbs in the Bible.

It's amazing that basic advice for living, written over 2000 years ago, can resound so clearly in our soul today. It's simple but not always easy!

You'll find a truth that penetrates your heart in a new way.

The path of wisdom results in the deep-seated peace and security you've been looking for.

You'll discover what the Book of Proverbs says about work, God, relationships, sex, friendships, booze, security, finances, fear, and many other topics that apply to your life right now.

Wisdom is timeless.

"For wisdom is far more valuable than rubies. Nothing you desire can compare with it." Proverbs 8:11

OPEN THE DOOR TO A LIFE OF WISDOM

Proverbs 1 – WHAT DOES "FEAR GOD" MEAN?

Read Proverbs 1.

"The fear of the Lord is the beginning of knowledge" Prov 1:7(a)   Also, Proverbs 9:10 says, "The fear of the Lord is the foundation of wisdom. Knowledge of the Holy One results in good judgment." What exactly is this "knowledge" and does it mean only smart people are wise? Do I need to be afraid of God to be wise?

This world is full of knowledge but there is a difference deep inside of us when we hear truth. The knowledge Proverbs talks about is much more than scientifically-conclusive data. It is not limited to super smart people. We're talking about knowledge directly related to the soul. This knowledge is buried deep in every person. Ecclesiastes 3:11 says, "He has planted eternity in the human heart." Repeat: This knowledge is hidden inside every single person. This is knowledge of truth. (Think of truth as a noun.)

Truth can only come from God. There is no other truth. Do you believe this? Or do you believe there are "many truths" or "to each his own" and "whatever is right for you is right and whatever is wrong for you is wrong?" Do you believe morality depends on the situation and the people involved? This is called moral relativism. The truth that is planted in each of us does not agree with this philosophy. Deep down inside we know it.

There's a lack of satisfaction in moral relativism and false wisdom. It doesn't quite touch that place inside each of us that desperately seeks fulfillment. It misses the mark.

In Proverbs, and throughout the Bible, God provides simple knowledge and wisdom for life that is based on truth. Anybody is able to follow the direction He provides. Absolutely anybody. He touches our soul and resonates in our hearts. We recognize truth at a gut level and it satisfies something inside of us.

We may not always like it, but we will always be transformed by it.

We must first get our head around who God is, and who we are to Him. This is important. Once we get that, then comes the fear, or reverence, for a holy and perfect God. "Fear of God" is a great example of a truth that is controversial.

Think about how you would feel in the presence of a human king or the president of the United States? Our hands would shake and we'd be awestruck by their presence. We would show this person great respect due to their position and power. Heck, we may feel this way around our boss. It's only natural.

God is the almighty, all-powerful ruler of the universe. It's ridiculous not to fear God!

Let this basic truth sink in before going any further. Remember, the fear of the Lord is the beginning of knowledge.

Now we are ready to receive knowledge.

Most of Proverbs 1 describes the consequences of a life lived foolishly. The second part of Verse 7 says fools hate knowledge. The fool does not fear God. As we go through Proverbs we see a fool's life story is painful, insecure, traumatic, and dark. It's full of bad choices and failed relationships.

A fool would likely revere a worldly king or president. A fool refuses to fear God. The fool may be a highly intelligent person full of worldly knowledge. The fool lacks wisdom.

Be careful. As we read about the fool we shouldn't get too cocky – at times the fool actually describes us!

Okay, this is going to get deep. If we are willing to be humble and fear God, Verse 33 concludes Proverbs 1 with the ultimate assurance: "But whoever listens to me will dwell safely and will dwell secure, without the fear of evil." Don't mistake this kind of fear with the fear of God. Evil is the absence of God. The bad kind of fear is the kind that paralyzes us and ruins lives. It's based on all kinds of lies. It's evil. Fear of God and fear of evil cannot exist together.

The more wisdom we attain, the less power fear has in our life. Can you imagine a life without fear?

Fear is the foundation of every kind of ugliness in our world. We make bad decisions out of fear and we miss out on life due to fear. Greed, selfishness, abuse, and self-centeredness are rooted in fear. At its worst, it's debilitating and deadly. Fear is everywhere and permeates our culture. It's like a black cloud over society, just watch the news.

Moral relativism breeds fear.

Nowhere in the Bible does it say we are to fear anything other than God. Remember how big God is? He's bigger than our fear and He protects us. Wisdom protects us! You'll see this commitment to protection throughout Proverbs. Once again, try to imagine a life without fear. That's what God wants. Fear has no place in a life of wisdom.

Although fear has infected our world, wisdom cries out loud in the streets to get our attention. Over and over Proverbs describes wisdom as a treasure to be desired above all. It is more precious than rubies, gold, silver, or any kind of cash. This is not a hidden treasure only for the elite, the ultra intelligent, or the gifted. Wisdom is for anybody willing to put God in His rightful place in their heart, mind, and life.

Fear of God is the beginning of knowledge and the foundation of wisdom. The more we get wisdom, the less we will fear. Our lives become stable, secure, and we can do so much more.

Let's get started.

Proverbs 2 – COMBATTING THE LIES

Read Proverbs 2.

Let's talk more about security. A life of wisdom brings deep and unshakeable security. This is one reason why wisdom is so valuable. It is more precious than gold and silver, but we have to do our part. We must pursue it.

Verses 1–3 use active words such as listen, tune your ears, concentrate, cry out, search, and seek. This is not a passive journey. In Jeremiah 29:3 it says, "God says you will seek me and find me when you seek me with your whole heart." The reward for our efforts is knowledge of God. Remember, knowledge of God gives us wisdom. Do you know where you get knowledge of God?

Proverbs 2:10 says, "For wisdom will enter your heart, and knowledge will fill you with joy."

Not only does knowledge of God give us joy, but He is a shield; He guards, protects, and keeps us safe. This is security we long for. Proverbs continuously shows how wisdom protects us from evil. It's like we have a force field around us that evil can't penetrate. We are resting in a new sense of security, but yet we are also traveling and moving in the right direction. Wisdom shows us the right way to go – ways that are straight. This also keeps us safe. Often in Proverbs the fool's path is described as crooked.

With wisdom and knowledge we make good life choices, and we are not influenced or deceived by evil. Make no mistake; the heart of evil is deception and lies. Fools are easily deceived because they hate truth and they lack the "soul knowledge" we've been talking about. It's pretty simple. Where can we actively seek this knowledge? (Hint: there's only one place in this world.)

Proverbs 1:16 starts to talk about the immoral woman and describes her ways. Stop for a minute and replace the image of an actual woman with the emotion of lust. Now read back through the verses with this in mind.

Lust is evil, self-centered, and leads to destruction and instability. We love lust in our society – it's everywhere. Even while all around us the consequences are painfully obvious, lust continues to be glorified.

Although it's truly ugly at its heart, lust always starts out with enticing and glamorous images, and smooth words. The lies. Our eyes are drawn to it and pride keeps it alive. When someone purposely pursues us lustfully with compliments and suggestive words, we can be easily tempted. This is why we walk a path of integrity and stay far from those situations. We don't hang out at bars, with married members of the opposite sex, or with people engaged in a promiscuous lifestyle. Wisdom guards us and gives us good judgment. We can no longer lie to ourselves.

Lust causes marriages to crumble and devastates families. It degrades both men and women, and undermines what God created to be beautiful. Evil loves lust. In order to pursue it, we must turn away from God. It brings instability to our youth. Kids are sexualized at a young age, bombarded with images and access. There is a boatload of insecurity that comes with the sin of lust. We must be wise in the way we protect and teach our children.

If we struggle with the emotion of lust, then we need to first see it for what it is: evil and ugly, and always a source of volatility. Some of us have a really hard time and battle inside with this issue. This is the battle between truth and the lie. Take heart, it's a war that's already been won...but we still get to choose which side we are on.

To combat all temptation is simple: turn away from it. James 4:7 says "So humble yourselves before God. Resist the devil, and he will flee from you." It's really that straightforward. Psalm 34:14 takes it another step. "Turn away from evil and do good; seek peace and pursue it." Take purposeful action. Another tool that works when we recognize temptation is to say, "I am dead to that." This agrees with Romans 6:11. It really works! So, turn away from it and rebuke it even if you don't feel like it. You just might be amazed at how much power you have inside. We just have to be willing to break away from the spell of the lie for a moment of sanity.

Talk about it...yes, out loud. It takes the power out of the temptation. If this is a serious issue for you, these are the things we

15

share with a mentor. Chances are they will understand. Time to get real. Your security is at stake.

Finally, with regard to security, Verses 21–22 give yet another level of insight into godly security. Imagine living in a place, settling down, and making a home where you know you are welcome, loved, and sheltered. This is a basic human need. Now imagine constantly being uprooted, unwelcome, with no place to live. Ever. Those who walk a path of wisdom, humility, and integrity feel safe and secure all the time, just like finding a true home.

It should be noted, our outward living conditions have little to do with our security. That being said, our outward circumstances will directly reflect our inner heart. The homes of wicked people are unstable and unsafe; the homes of the wise are a sanctuary and a place we want to be. It's a safe place free from evil and trauma.

Godly wisdom keeps us far from treacherous and crooked paths in life. We follow the steps of good men and women, and enjoy security and peace. It's not complicated but it's not always easy. It always boils back down to that crazy humble thing again… you know, where God is huge and we are not. God will give us His strength and it's crucial that we rely on Him to defeat the evil and fear in our lives.

Proverbs 3 – TRUST AND LET GO

Read Proverbs 3.

As we study Proverbs 3 we find relief and comfort to realize we don't have to rely on what we know. We are limited in our knowledge, but God knows everything. He literally knows every single thing – do you believe that? This includes the future. He's already been there! Psalm 139 goes into great detail describing how much God knows about us personally. It's to the point of obsession. Take the time now to go read it like a passionate love letter from Him directly to you.

Do you feel adored? You should. God is possessive of you, and He is absolutely, one hundred percent good. There is no evil in Him and there is no darkness in Him. He wants you in a way that is more intimate than you could ever realize. He wants to be in your head. He wants to dwell in your body. He wants to own your heart. Yikes! It's almost stalkerish ... except He is purely good.

Consider the fact that He already knows your future. He definitely cares about it. Do you believe this? Maybe you agree with Psalm 139:6 where it says, "such knowledge is too wonderful and too high to attain." That's okay too. At the very least, have faith and trust that He knows your future. In fact, trust it blindly.

Blind trust is something that defies worldly "knowledge." It's much more logical to put God in a box where we can better understand Him and control Him. Right? That doesn't even make sense.

Proverbs 3:5-6 says to, "Trust in the Lord with all your heart; do not depend on your own understanding. Seek His will in all you do, and He will show you which path to take." This is an excellent verse to memorize and keep in your back pocket for times of uncertainty. It will bring you right smack back to the present moment.

Our understanding is very limited. His is not. Trust Him. Let go of the control. Men can struggle sometimes with the instruction to trust God completely. They are usually wired to take charge and take responsibility. These verses are about letting go of outcomes. We are limited in what we know about any situation.

The challenge is to hand the reins to Him in all things. All. He will guide us and we need to leave the results to Him. If this is hard for you, try baby steps. Think of something you can fathom letting go of and try it. Practice letting go and trusting God with this one little thing. Watch and see what happens. The experience will build your faith as God works His will in the situation.

Sometimes we have no idea what is going on when life throws us a curveball. Maybe we've lost a job, a loved one dies, or a relationship has gone sideways. We feel lost, scared, and confused. These are the times where it's easy to lean not on our own understanding. We really don't understand! During these times,

18

pull Proverbs 3:5-6 out of that back pocket and experience the comfort that only comes from the truth. You'll find yourself staying in the moment when you stop freaking out about the future.

Proverbs has a lot to say about riches and 3:9-10 instructs us to honor God with our wealth, and the reward is abundance and plenty. Practically speaking, debt and foolish financial decisions prevent us from honoring God with our wealth. It also prevents us from being prosperous. We're too darn busy trying to get caught up!

What does it mean to honor God with our wealth? Back in Verse 6 it says, "In all your ways acknowledge Him." (NASB) This includes our money. We need to start to see God as our provider. It's not our job, our business, the government, or our spouse. He provides our income and our wealth. This is an awesome truth to meditate on in order to deepen your sense of security. This is one way we honor God with our wealth, by acknowledging it's all from Him. When we really understand that He is our provider, we no longer feel insecure about money. He is a faithful provider.

Pretty soon we are feeling compelled to give to others who are in need. Go with it.

Verses 27 and 28 tell us not to hesitate if we have the power to help another person. We find one of the key characteristics of God's wisdom is the emphasis He places on helping the poor. This is another way we honor God with our finances. The more prosperous we are, the more we are able to give generously.

19

The more secure we are in God's provision, the less we cling to money and the more generous we become. If we cling to wealth, we become insecure and are less generous.

Finally, the security thing keeps cropping up. Once again Verses 24 through 26 reflect a life of peace, stability, and fearlessness. "You will not be afraid, your sleep will be sweet, you will not be afraid of sudden disaster."

The Lord is our security and fear has no place in the life of a believer. When God is big and we are small we can sleep soundly in the arms of one who loves us with an all-consuming obsession. Go back and read Psalm 139. Now contemplate the truth that He is your provider.

Proverbs 4 – SOMEONE TO GET REAL WITH

Read Proverbs 4.

The good news is wisdom can be taught! Like we talked about before, it's not for the specially gifted. It's for anybody willing to learn. Verse 11 says, "I have taught you the way of wisdom."

The fourth book of Proverbs continues with a theme of following instruction and good guidance. The Proverbs are directed toward "my son" or "my child" and are from a father's perspective. He implores the child to listen, pay attention, take his words to heart, follow, and don't forget. He was taught by his father and desires to pass on wisdom for life to his kid.

Not everybody was blessed by a wise father at birth. You can be assured you have a Heavenly Father who created wisdom and loves you. He will lead you. He pretty much always uses other people. Our elders are wise and can teach us what they have learned. With good judgment that comes from God we learn to follow the right advice.

Verse 18 describes the wise life beautifully. It is like the first light of dawn which shines brighter and brighter until the full light of day. As we age, the light of God shines brighter.

If you don't have one, pray for a mentor and accountability partner to be brought into your life. Seek someone who has a life you admire, respect, and a person you can trust implicitly. This is super important. Pray and wait to see what God does.

If you have a grandparent or an elderly person in your life that loves God, rejoice! Seek this person's company often and regularly. They have much to offer and they will cherish your company.

When you are in pain you can feel alone. That's another lie to keep you stuck. You are not alone. There are always other people who have been through the same thing and have come out the other side healed and whole. God can put those people in your life to help you heal. If you don't know where to find these people, try doing some research into support groups and mentorship programs.

Be aware there is a lot of false wisdom out there. True biblical wisdom from God satisfies and heals our soul. We don't want little Band-Aids. We want permanent healing. Be sure you are spiritually aligned with any mentors.

Now we're ready to help others.

Everybody has hurt. Use your brokenness as something very important to share with others. God will put those people in your life so you can help them heal. Helping others will deepen your healing as well. This is the heart of the command to "Love your neighbor as yourself." (Galatians 5:14)

God gets us. He knows what we need.

Worldly council will direct people to dwell on their past and to focus on their childhood for answers. They may say things like "get in touch with your inner child." In Verse 25 God says to look straight ahead and fix your eyes on what lies before you. Don't spend a bunch of time living in the past. Key word: living.

The healing that comes with biblical wisdom is permanent and transforming. Romans 12:2 tells us, "Do not be conformed to this world, but be transformed by the renewal of your mind." The renewal referred to is what happens when we study the Bible. It's an amazing and supernatural experience that happens over time. As we heal we become emotionally free to leave the past behind.

Yes, of course, sometimes we have work to do dealing with past hurts. Dealing with our past, and living in the past, are two vastly different concepts. A lot is accomplished by talking about it out loud, forgiveness, and letting go. These are the things we work through (out loud) with a wise mentor. Remember, wisdom can be taught.

We leave the past behind and we don't worry about the future – remember, you only have limited information. Go back to Proverbs 3:5-6. Stay in today, in this moment. Jesus said in Matthew 6:34, "So don't worry about tomorrow, for tomorrow will bring its own worries. Today's trouble is enough for today."

Have you ever noticed how kids naturally stay in the present moment? As we grow out of childhood we lose this gift. Many of us are blessed with magical and vivid memories of childhood. Memories of Christmases, camping trips, summer afternoons, tree forts, and family vacations are firmly rooted in our memories. (Note: having memories and dwelling in the past are not the same.)

When we practice living in the moment, our future memories of these current moments become rich and colorful. Even when the times are hard, these memories are more meaningful. It's because we are present.

A sure way to bring yourself into the moment is to completely let go of everything in your heart and trust God. Like a child.

Life is way too short not to be right smack in the middle of it at all times!

We need people in our life we can trust. Sometimes life is hard, and it's a comfort to have others who love us and can help guide us. God made us this way. He wants to use others and he wants to use you. We are meant to live life together. Today is the day to seek out those people before difficulties come.

Proverbs 5 – BAD SEX AND GOOD SEX

Read Proverbs 5.

Proverbs 5 focuses heavily on the immoral woman. Once again, instead of the image of an actual woman, we will look at the emotion of lust in general. It's relevant and helps provide deeper insight. This takes the focus off some bad lady and back on to us.

Most adults have probably experienced the sin of lust. Yes, it is a sin. It misses the mark of God's perfect standard. God created sex. Lust is not from God. It starts out smooth and sweet like honey, but in the end always leads to destruction.

Back in Proverbs 4:19 it says the way of the wicked is in complete darkness and they don't even know what they're stumbling over. Proverbs 5:6 specifically points to lust's crooked and treacherous path. Verses 7 and 8 are a begging plea to say away from lust. Don't go near her. Just like we talked about in chapter 2, turn away and keep moving. Resist the Devil and he will flee. Say out loud, "I'm dead to that."

The consequences of entertaining lust are serious and destructive to life. Usually multiple lives are affected. As pointed out throughout Proverbs 5, loss of honor, loss of wealth, disease consumes the body, utter ruin, and public disgrace. Even when we're not "caught" the destruction takes place.

Pursuing lust creates internal destruction and hard heartedness that blocks God from working for our good. The ultimate consequence of sin is spiritual death. All of this is due to lack of self-control and great foolishness.

Verse 21 reminds us that the, "Lord sees clearly what a man does, examining every path he takes." God is studying you all the time. Nothing is hidden. Deep inside we know this. In our sin and guilt we turn away from God so we don't have to face Him.

Lust is a lie and when the act is complete we are left with shame and emptiness. Repeat: we are left with shame and emptiness. Every. Single. Time. How many times do we need to experience this to finally turn away?

In contrast, Verses 15 through 19 echoes the language of the Bible's romantic love song – The Song of Solomon. It discusses sharing a beautiful love with your spouse. The sensual words in describing the wife are pure and use images of nature.

God created sex as a deeply spiritual and natural act between a man and a woman. He purposely made it pleasurable for humans. In describing marriage He says in Mark 10:8, "and the two are united into one. Since they are no longer two but one." This is directly related to the intimate purpose of sex. You become one flesh with another in the act of sex.

The question is asked in Proverbs why sex would be shared with just anyone. (Verse 20) 1 Corinthians 6:16 says, "and don't you realize that if a man joins himself to a prostitute, he becomes one body with her? For the Scriptures say, 'The two are united into one.'" In this chapter of Proverbs it's compared to spilling pure water from your private spring into the gutter. It doesn't make sense and it's a waste.

God created sex to be a bonding act between a husband and a wife. He is so serious about it that He has declared that sex creates one flesh between two people. When He created woman, He made her from the flesh of man. (Genesis 2:22) This is why casual sex goes against everything God created it to be.

It's especially difficult for single people. God also gave us a sex drive and when we get lonely it amplifies the need for that natural bonding He created in us. The best thing to do is focus your mind away from sex during this season of life. It is very important to seek wisdom and seek companionship with people you trust. Surround yourself with people you know love you, and pour your energy into serving others. Seriously, that really works! You'll be amazed how intense service work can completely turn your focus away from your unfulfilled need. It also gives God time to send you a worthy mate. Seek ways to volunteer and pray all the time. Cry when you need to. It's okay.

If you're married and passion for your spouse has faded, there is hope. It may take counseling and it will require honesty and hard work. It definitely requires willingness, obedience, and effort. Start today.

Pay attention to your thoughts of your spouse. Nip the negative thoughts in the bud and stop picking him apart! List all of the things you like about your spouse. What is cute and attractive about her? What attracted you in the first place? Repeat these things in your mind. Desire has less to do with the outside and more to do with our attitude. With God there is always hope. He promises renewal.

Maybe you've just created a bad habit in your marriage of not making sex a priority. It's important to both of you, but you find weeks or even months go by without sex. That's not healthy. Make a commitment to do it regularly whether you want it or not! This is said tongue in cheek, of course. We almost always find once we start we enjoy it and are always glad we did it. Sometimes just the fact that we did it feels just as satisfying as the physical aspect. We know we did something good for our relationship.

Sex is meant to be healing for a marriage. Make it a priority and put in the effort. Date nights, putting the kids to bed early, marking it on the calendar, add some spice. Do whatever works for you and have fun with it. It's important.

If you have desire for your spouse, rejoice! The Bible gives some vital council for sex in marriage: "Do not deprive each other of sexual relations, unless you both agree. Afterward, you should come together again so that Satan won't be able to tempt you because of your lack of self-control." (1 Corinthians 7:5) It's very important to maintain an active and loving sex life. It brings supernatural healing

28

to your marriage.   Next time you make love, realize that you are one flesh with your spouse.

Jesus understands our weaknesses.   The night before He went to the cross He told His disciples, "Keep watch and pray, so that you will not give in to temptation. For the spirit is willing, but the body is weak." (Matthew 26:41)

If you're struggling in this area, know that we can get through anything with God's strength and love.   Be vigilant and be aware of your thoughts in this area.   Pray and use the tools we've talked about.

Proverbs 6 – HIGH STANDARDS

Read Proverbs 6.

Proverbs has a lot of wisdom on work ethic – or lack thereof. This must be a very important topic to God. He cares about our work, and for most of us it's an area of life that consumes a majority of our time.

In Proverbs 6:7-8 the ant is used as the example of productivity. "Though they have no prince or governor or ruler to make them work, they labor hard all summer, gathering food for the winter." Ants work hard and don't require supervision. They are prepared for times of scarcity. They are also well-known for carrying more than their weight. Literally.

Even if you are temporarily unemployed there are always opportunities to be productive. There is volunteer work, projects around the house, and the job of finding a job.

The contrast to productivity is the lazybones who is always napping.

People who sleep a lot are never prosperous in Proverbs. It's an excellent practice to wake up early every day. Even if you're naturally a night owl, manage your sleep habits. Proverbs 31:15 describes one of the most industrious people in the Bible and she rises early every morning. It just makes sense.

Imagine a successful person you know and whether or not they would lay in bed until noon – even on a Saturday. Productivity and preparedness are attributes of wealth and wisdom. Laziness is not. Besides that, hard work feels good at the basic core of who we are.

Productivity is particularly important if we work for someone else providing our paycheck. We owe them a good day's work to earn our keep. Otherwise, it's stealing. If we work for ourselves we'll reap the rewards of our work ethic – which is extremely gratifying and motivating.

This work ethic concept is also true of the work we have at home. There is always plenty of work to do! In fact, our work ethic becomes quite visible just by looking at the way our home is kept up.

We can probably hide a poor work ethic at work (for awhile), but not at home. Dishes pile up, laundry takes over, and messes quickly ensue.

We know how much time we waste laying in bed, watching TV, playing video games, or surfing the net and we know how we feel inside.

It's vital for our mental and spiritual health to be productive!

One trick that seems to work if you're surrounded by clutter is to say out loud five times, "a place for everything and everything in its place." For some reason this works. Next thing we know we're picking up and putting things away, and feel a drive to bring order to chaos.

God is a God of harmony and order. Isaiah 45:8 says, "For the LORD is God, and he created the heavens and earth and put everything in place. He made the world to be lived in, not to be a place of empty chaos. 'I am the LORD,' he says, 'and there is no other.'" It's not a stretch to conceive that chaos is associated with evil. Observe a riot sometime. There is a lot to be said for making our beds every single day. A wise person once said that he makes his bed every day because even if his room is a mess it doesn't look quite as messy. It's just a good habit of orderliness.

The bottom line is, if we want to be prosperous we need to be productive. Simple daily habits add up.

Along the same lines, it's safe to say, how we live is a direct reflection of our spiritual condition. In Matthew 7:20 Jesus said, "Yes, just as you can identify a tree by its fruit, so you can identify people by their actions."

Along with laziness, it becomes clear God hates some things in Proverbs 6. In Verses 16 through 19 we actually get a list of the top seven things NOT to do:

1. Don't be stuck up

2. Don't lie

3. Don't kill the innocent (p.s. God hates abortion)

4. Don't plot evil in your heart

5. Don't race to do wrong

6. Don't lie about somebody else

7. Don't stir up drama

We've all probably done some, or all, of these things that God hates. He knows that. Thankfully, He loves you and will never give up on you. That's why in Verses 20–22 in today's Proverb, He implores us to listen, seek, and keep His words in our heart. His word is the Bible. He wants it in our heart and mind. The Bible will counsel, advise, protect, lead, and instruct us in the way of wisdom.

He will help us not to do those things He hates. We have nothing to hide from God. When He comes first in our life, we grow to hate what He hates and love what He loves.

Let's look at the opposites of the bad list:

1. Be humble and approachable

2. Tell the truth

3. Protect and defend the innocent (be a hero and champion!)

4. Plot and plan good in your heart

5. Race to do good things – don't hesitate

6. Tell the truth

7. Be a peacemaker in your family.

It's safe to assume God loves these things. Clearly, honesty is crucial to our walk of wisdom. It's listed twice! We continue to realize none of these things are complicated – they're just not always easy.

It's about a life of integrity. It sounds so simple but it can be uncommon. As we grow every day for the rest of our lives in our walk with God, we strive for perfection. Not in a way that makes us feel less-than, but in a way that we become transformed.

We should be full of hope that this is a lifelong process and that we actually do have high standards! Keep looking forward, but also celebrate the changes that have happened inside of you.

When it comes to striving for God's perfection the Bible says, "Let all who are spiritually mature agree on these things. If you disagree on some point, I believe God will make it plain to you. But we must hold on to the progress we have already made" (Philippians 3: 15-16). We agree that, yes, we are striving for God's perfection in our lives. It is extremely important to note that God's perfection includes grace and forgiveness.

If you are not yet spiritually mature, trust those who are. This is a process that brings freedom not condemnation. It's a labor of love. Hopefully you're starting to experience it as you embrace the highest standards!

Proverbs 7 – HIDE YOUR EYES

Read Proverbs 7.

The first verses continue to implore us to take the commands and wise instruction deep into our hearts. (Verse 7) You probably already know this, but the Bible is where we attain knowledge of God. It's why He gave it to us and it contains his instructions to us.

Before reading your Bible, pray some version of the following prayer: "God, please let your word penetrate supernaturally and deeply into my heart, mind, body, and soul". Hold it precious.

Verse 1 says to treasure these commands, as if something were so priceless that we would guard it with extreme care and tend to it regularly. In fact, Verse 2 says to, "guard these instructions as you would guard your own eyes." When we place a high value on God's word it will change our life and it changes the way we see things.

If our eyes were damaged, it would have a devastating impact on our lives. Most of us are heavily reliant on sight and instinctively protect our eyes.

Just as we naturally guard our physical eyes, we learn to guard the truth with the same impulse. We start to recognize lies and immediately shield ourselves from them. This is called discernment.

As a parallel lesson, what we physically look at impacts the direction of our life. Proverbs 23:26 says, "My son, give me your heart and let your eyes delight in my ways."

Pornography is an example where our eyes are not being protected. By the same token, gazing at and admiring a member of the opposite sex, even fully clothed, can create emotions that lead us down wayward paths based on lust or fantasy. We've already established the pitfalls of lust. It starts with our thoughts, and thoughts can be prompted by what we look at. Visual cues are powerful. We need to immediately stop and avert our eyes.

A pastor once told how he had to change the way he drove to the church every day. His normal road to work went past a bikini barista stand. He found his eyes being drawn to the stand when he drove past. Because it bugged him, it created an inner conflict and the best way to deal with it was to avoid it. This might seem ridiculous to our culture, so calloused to promiscuity, but it's wise. This is an example of what guarding our eyes looks like.

Television, movies, media, and billboards - lust is everywhere in our society. Within a few generations we have gone from modesty to blatant sexuality, and quite honestly, degradation. Homosexuality and casual sex are being driven into our culture as normal and perfectly acceptable. In fact, people who are opposed to these "values" are considered wrong and even hateful. There is unprecedented access to pornography through the internet. Children are exposed to sex at a very young age and it's damaging their souls.

We must protect our children's eyes. This should be a no-brainer. By protecting their eyes we're protecting their hearts, minds, and souls. It's important!

We do this through monitoring all media interaction. There are a lot of practical resources out there to help us with that. At the same time, we are aware of their activities, friends, and whereabouts. We ensure our daughters dress appropriately and we teach our sons about respecting girls. A truly loving parent will continue this practice while a child is well into their teens. They may not like it, but deep inside they'll feel safe and secure because you love them in the same way God loves you.

As women, we need to honestly look at the way we present ourselves and our motives. Is it to entice men or a particular man? This is a major danger zone. Enticement, seduction, and temptation are the hallmarks of the immoral woman portrayed throughout Proverbs. She thrives on purposely inciting lust.

We absolutely do not want to encourage the emotion of lust. This may be a hard thing for us to face.

Our society glorifies "sexiness" and we can find ourselves feeling ugly and insignificant. We compare ourselves to perfect airbrushed images, or even to women who openly flaunt their sexuality, and see men flock to it. We feel like a wallflower.

The truth sets us free. The truth is we want to feel beautiful on the inside, and that's exactly what we're doing as we seek wisdom. It's the only truly satisfying and sustained beauty. It is also extremely attractive to good men.

The truth is, when men look at women with lust, it is a self-centered motive that has nothing to do with the core of who you are. You are an object. In other words, the inside is meaningless.

The truth is, at the bikini barista stand these women put up with the vilest of men making passes at them. They are leered at and we don't even want to know what guys say behind their backs. It feels ugly.

Blatantly flaunting our sexuality starts a cycle of inner ugliness that causes us to take it further and further. Our insecurity creates more cleavage and shorter skirts which feeds the ugliness inside. It's not good!

Ladies, this is a huge and important topic that we'll cover in deeper detail at a later time. Just know this, once you experience being loved and cherished as a woman, you'll never settle for anything less. It would be like tossing pearls to swine. (Matthew 7:6)

Men need to dare to be different too. Don't toss your pearls to swine either! Just as Proverbs has shown, see lust for what it is; a lie that destroys lives. Your virility and sexuality are a gift from God and you are made in His image. Recognize where you may look at women as sex objects and get real with God about it. Work with a strong male mentor and hold yourself accountable to him. Talk about your thought life. If you struggle with pornography, get honest and bring it out into the light. If the thoughts come into your mind that starts the pattern, focus your thoughts on how you feel after the act is over. Guilt and emptiness are ultimately the end result. Let's repeat that: guilt and emptiness are ultimately the end result. Use the tools we talked about previously; turn away, rebuke it, and take action in another direction. Say out loud, "I'm dead to that." Another tactic, if you have daughters, should be easy; imagine if a man looked at or treated your daughter in these ways. The bottom line is, in order to be at peace and live the life God intends, you can't nurture lust.

Overall, both men and women should cherish wisdom and be very protective of the truth. As we grow in wisdom and knowledge we start to love what God loves and hate what God hates. We also reap the benefits of such a life. You'll create a safe and secure environment for you and those closest to you. In the Book of John 8:32 Jesus says, "and you will know the truth and the truth shall set you free." In John 8:34 Jesus clarifies what He means by that; "Jesus replied, 'I tell you the truth, everyone who sins is a slave of sin.'" We don't have to be slaves.

Let the truth set you free.

Proverbs 8 – THE THROBBING HEART OF WISDOM

Read Proverbs 8.

Proverbs 8 provides deep insight into the heart of wisdom. Wisdom is obvious and everywhere. Wisdom wants to be known and every single person has access to her. Wisdom shouts out, she calls to us.

Over and over again throughout Proverbs it says wisdom brings prosperity and success. Not all lovers and seekers of wisdom will get rich by the world's standards, but those who pursue wisdom receive something more valuable than rubies. (Verse 11) It's better than purest gold and silver. (Verse 19)

Nothing you desire can compare to the satisfaction that comes from a life of wisdom.

Verse 32 through 35 says those who follow the path of seeking wisdom are joyful. Wisdom doesn't come and seek us, by the way. She makes herself very available and it is our responsibility to seek, search, listen, follow, find, watch, and wait.

The security that comes with wisdom can never be taken away. Jesus said in Matthew 6:20, "Store your treasures in heaven, where moths and rust cannot destroy, and thieves do not break in and steal." A life well lived will produce much treasure. With wisdom we look at life with an eternal perspective and become less dependent on people, places, or things of this world to make us feel secure.

No power on Earth can take wisdom away from you. We've talked a lot about the benefits of wisdom: safety, security, prosperity, peace. This is worth dwelling on.

In this chapter we also receive insight into wisdom's origins. She was formed from the beginning by God before He created anything else. Wisdom was by His side as He joyfully created the heavens and earth. Verse 30 says wisdom was the architect at His side.

It goes on to say wisdom was God's constant delight and she rejoiced always in His presence. This tells us that God delights when we rejoice in His presence as well. Take a moment right now to stop and simply rejoice in your relationship with a God who cares so deeply and intimately for you. He is with you now.

Verse 31 shows the heart of wisdom in relation to us humans, "And happy I was with the world He created; how I rejoiced with the human family." That's amazing. Obviously wisdom is directly aligned with God's will for us.

Wisdom comes from God and is one with God. Wisdom does not originate with humans. It is a supernatural quality and there is a humble royalty associated with it. And to think it is ours if we simply seek, search, listen, follow, obey, find, watch, and wait. That is what you are doing at this moment.

Why would anybody not love wisdom? In Verse 17 wisdom says, "I love all who love me." What a great chapter to re-motivate us on this journey of seeking wisdom. At this point, it seems ludicrous that there would be any other way to live! There seems to be no downside and all upside. This is how God intended it from the beginning.

Make no mistake, the world is confused about what is desirable and what is not. We talk over and again that this journey is simple but not easy. Those of us who oppose immorality are viewed as intolerant and hateful. James 4:4 tells it like it is and says, "friends of the world are enemies of God." Proverbs 8 concludes in Verse 36 stating that those who hate wisdom love death. As you grow in wisdom you become an alien in this world, and a threat to the worldly values that oppose God. You are Satan's enemy and he will attack you over and over again. How do you feel about that? Does it scare you? Remember what we learned about this kind of fear; it has no place in a life of wisdom.

We remain secure that we have received treasures that can never be taken away. As it says in Romans 8:39, nothing can separate us from the love of God: "No power in the sky above or in the earth below--indeed, nothing in all creation will ever be able to separate us from the love of God who is revealed in Christ Jesus our Lord." Wisdom is a treasured gift from God, let's cherish it.

Proverbs 9 – COME TO THE PARTY!

Read Proverbs 9.

Proverbs 9 is short and sweet. Verses 1 through 7 portray an open invitation for anyone and everyone. Even the fool and those who lack good judgment are not excluded from the party. Wisdom does everything possible to ensure everybody is invited. The invitation includes a great banquet, wine, servants, and a wide open door.

Imagine a time you had a party and how you were so focused on the guests. You wanted them to feel welcome, be comfortable, and enjoy themselves in your house. You were excited and wanted everything to be perfect. The preparations took days and the whole time the guests were on your mind. Maybe there was a new friend you wanted to feel particularly welcome. This is how God feels about us and our pursuit of wisdom. He is celebrating every victory.

To the fool He says in Verse 7, "leave your simple ways behind and begin to live. Learn to use good judgment." Wisdom is not a gift that suddenly and magically appears. We've already established that it requires effort on our part. It's also a process that we learn and build upon. It starts when we accept the invitation to participate.

There are several parables in the Book of Luke where Jesus talks about how God celebrates over every single lost person who is found. In Luke 15:7 it describes this celebration throughout heaven;

"In the same way, there is more joy in heaven over one lost sinner who repents and returns to God, than over ninety-nine others who are righteous and haven't strayed away!"

Verse 10 reminds us again that fear of the Lord is the foundation of wisdom and knowledge. Let's celebrate the freedom and peace we've found in wisdom.

Proverbs 10 - WORDS, WISDOM, AND WEALTH

Read Proverbs 10.

You may notice chapter 10 changes things up. There begins a series of contrasts between good and bad behavior and their results. There are plenty of points of wisdom about words we use.

Proverbs is full of common sense that is uncommon. For example, Verse 19 says, "Too much talk leads to sin. Be sensible and keep your mouth shut." For those of us who talk too much we understand this advice. The Bible has a lot to say about the power of the tongue – Google it sometime.

Needless to say, lives can be destroyed or transformed by words.

Over in Proverbs 17:28 it says, "Even fools are thought wise when they keep silent; with their mouths shut, they seem intelligent." (That's actually kind of funny.)

If you are someone who always has to get your two cents in on conversations, do an experiment sometime and keep silent. Hopefully we find that we are actually listening. It is a major exercise in self-control, which is always a good thing. Good listeners are attractive, humble, and charming people. They are perceived as more trustworthy and wise.

On the other hand, wisdom says "a bold reproof promotes peace". If a good friend or family member is dealing with consequences of living a foolish life, it seems easier to talk about them, than talk to them in a bold and honest way.

There are very few things more impactful than when someone who loves us tells us the truth about how we're messing up. In Proverbs 6:27 it says, "Wounds from a sincere friend are better than many kisses from an enemy."

These types of experiences lead to feelings of conviction. Real change doesn't happen unless we are truly convicted, or convinced. It's the truth gnawing at our conscience. The Holy Spirit causes these feelings. Wisdom and the Holy Spirit are linked. As we grow spiritually, conviction becomes passion. We also experience the freedom of a clear conscience!

Think of the times when you've been "talked to" at work about unacceptable behavior. You remember it well, it was humbling, and it usually caused a change in behavior. Maybe you've had other turning points in your life due to a bold reproof. Some of us may have heard a sermon from the Bible that caused us to finally face the truth about our lifestyle. Those are the words that change lives.

Messages that co-sign or justify our sins don't cause true change that brings peace.

The words of the godly are a life-giving fountain (Verse 11), they are like sterling silver (Verse 20), and encourage many (Verse

21). People need our words. We give good advice and speak helpful words…even when it's hard.

Words also reveal characteristics of the wicked. Verse 6 says, "They conceal violent intentions." Swearing and cussing are considered abusive language. Do you notice how you feel when you cuss too much or you're around someone who curses a lot. There is an underlying violence and anger in swearing. Some of us need to continue to work on not being a fool in this area. Chances are there may be anger issues behind the habit of swearing.

There are also contrasts between work ethic and wealth in Proverbs 10. Very concisely Verse 4 simply states "lazy people are soon poor; hard workers get rich". There are no get rich schemes in the Bible. There are not many lazy rich people who stay rich.

Conversely, Verse 15 says the wealth of the rich is his fortress and the poverty of the fool is his destruction. Neither of these are good! Elsewhere Proverbs 30:9 says, "For if I grow rich, I may deny you and say, 'Who is the LORD?' And if I am too poor, I may steal and thus insult God's holy name." Being too rich is not good and being too poor is not good.

If you've ever been in a position where you have large amounts of wealth, you know how much more difficult it is to trust God. We start to trust the wealth. We think it keeps us safe. That is why there is great wisdom throughout Proverbs in giving to the poor. It's also wise to meditate on the truth that it all comes from God. He has provided it to you to take good care of and manage it well.

Most likely if we are wise we will increase our material wealth. The important thing is to place our security in God. We need to pray to have a heart that is willing to let go of all of it. Let go of the ownership. This becomes extremely difficult the more we have.

Those under financial impoverishment are operating on fear which is the opposite of faith. We also know this type of fear does not come from God. Many acts of desperation come when people are destitute and they are unable to have faith that their needs are being cared for. If you feel you are in that position, read through the book of Psalms and underline all the verses where God says He will care for you and provide for you. There are a lot. Faith will replace your fear. Do the next right thing, be wise and trust Him to be your provider. He is faithful even when we're not.

A great verse to remember is Verse 16 where it flat out tells us if we are wise, our earnings will enhance our lives, but the evil squander money on sin.

Our spiritual condition is evident in the words we speak, our attitudes about wealth and how we spend money. In all cases it's a heart issue and self-control is the key.

Proverbs 11 – HUMILITY, HUMILIATION, AND GOODNESS

Read Proverbs 11.

In this chapter of Proverbs there are contrasts between good and evil, and their consequences. Verse 2 talks about humility and pride. As always, this is an excellent topic for those in pursuit of wisdom. It's also something we need to continuously study and meditate upon.

Pride leads to disgrace, but with humility comes wisdom. In our heart and mind, pride makes us huge and God small. God becomes very distant. Ego could easily stand for "edging God out." When we are huge our perspectives become the opposite of wise. We start to rely on our own knowledge to make decisions. We think very highly of our abilities and hold ourselves in greater esteem than others. Next thing we know, our decisions are self-centered, self-serving, and the primary focus is "what is in it for me."

We have stopped pursing wisdom because we are so in love with how awesome we are.

In the Parable of the Guest in Luke 14:8-10, Jesus tells about not putting yourself in a place of honor unless you want to be asked to move out of the way. Instead, put yourself in a place of humbleness and you will be asked to come up and be honored.

49

Let's say you positioned yourself at the right hand of the host. Can you imagine the humiliation of being asked, in front of a crowd, to get out of your seat to make room for somebody more important? On the other hand, imagine being asked by the host to come up to the front to a place of honor. "Pride goes before destruction, and haughtiness before a fall" Proverbs 16:18.

Humility is truly the foundation of wisdom. By remembering who God is, and who we are in relation to Him, we naturally become humble. It requires commitment to daily stop, become quiet, understand God through His Word and meditate on the truth. We are back to revering God. Once again He's huge and we're tiny.

It's amazing that the almighty, all-powerful God of all creation, places such a high value on humility. Carefully read the words and meditate for a minute on Isaiah 57:15, "The high and lofty one who lives in eternity, the Holy One, says this: "'I live in the high and holy place with those whose spirits are contrite and humble." God hangs out with humble people.

This is not the world's value system. It is true wisdom. Jesus was, literally, the perfect example of humility. He was one with God in heaven since time began and before all eternity. He willingly came to Earth to walk with mankind and gave up His very life for those who would simply believe. (John 3:16) What kind of God is this? He defies logic.

There is enormous power in getting on our knees. If you are struggling with pride you will not be excited about this experiment; every day for seven days get on your knees and ask God to show you wisdom. Surely He will lovingly listen to any other prayers you may want to say.

Another way to break the bonds of selfishness and self-centeredness is to pray for others. Simply by the mental exercise of thinking of the needs of others, and lifting them up in prayer, deflates our ego.

Gratitude is incredibly important and powerful in our spiritual walk of wisdom. Be grateful every day. It's humbling and it feels good. It will instantly cheer you up. A sign of spiritual maturity is when our gratitude automatically goes to God, rather than a vague statement of gratitude. Thank God. Even greater maturity and joy is demonstrated when we are able to thank God for the difficulties and trials of life.

This advice is not something you see in the world. These practices, which line up with Scripture, change us from the inside out.

Finally, another great perspective-check for us is Proverbs 11:27; it says to, "search for good and you will find it." It's easy to find evil. If our minds are focused on evil we will find it. Philippians 4:8 is an excellent verse on this topic: "And now, dear brothers and sisters, one final thing. Fix your thoughts on what is true, and honorable, and right, and pure, and lovely, and admirable. Think about things that are excellent and worthy of praise".

Focus your mind on good. Remember we must guard our eyes. This also means focusing our mind on the things that are wholesome and pure. It's not that easy to do! Try identifying those things that represent the list in Philippians 4:8 above. It's another good spiritual exercise.

Don't dwell on the ugliness and don't look for it. We don't deny evil exists. That would be unwise. We just don't give it power in our lives.

None of this comes naturally to us and that is why we need God. It's no mistake that what God desires for you is not easy, but doesn't the truth resonate within your heart right now? The rewards are a rich and satisfying life of peace and humble honor.

Proverbs 12 – LIFE PLANS AND PET CARE

Read Proverbs 12.

God cares deeply about our thought life and the plans we make. The plans of the godly are just. (Verse 5) At the same time James 4:14-15 says, "how do you know what your life will be like tomorrow? Your life is like the morning fog--it's here a little while, then it's gone. What you ought to say is, "If the Lord wants us to, we will live and do this or that."

Let's be sure to always commit our plans to God and trust that His will is best. If we are worried that God's will isn't as good as ours, we need to keep reading our Bible and this book!

Deceit fills hearts that are plotting evil; joy fills hearts that are planning peace! (Verse 20)

What does plotting evil look like? It's easy to use examples such as murderers, rapists, and other villains. But just maybe it's a little closer to home.

The emotion of revenge is the equivalent of plotting evil. Harboring a grudge toward someone entails plotting evil in our heart. A decision to have an abortion, playing hooky from work by lying to the boss, sexual fantasies of someone other than a spouse, or on things we know are wrong. It has to do with our thought life. It's important that we are aware of the thoughts running through our minds. It's been said the mind is where the battle starts. Engaging in evil plans requires that we shut God out. This is the core of the deception referred to in Verse 20. At the very least, we justify our plans and pretend that God is fine with it.

Can you imagine choosing an abortion while on your knees praying to God? His plans would be different. He has plans for that baby. (If you've had an abortion, God loves you deeply. If you have repented you are absolutely one hundred percent forgiven. There will always be anguish but there is no condemnation in Christ Jesus. You can be comforted to know that your baby is in heaven and you will see that child one day.)

We've already established that nothing is hidden from God. We've also been shown that the truth is inside each one of us. In order to plan to continue lifestyle choices that are wrong, we must shut God out. The result becomes a hard heart. A hard-hearted person is one who absolutely refuses to fear God.

Many of the hardest-hearted people have eventually landed on their knees and God is always, always, always faithful to forgive. "But if we confess our sins to him, he is faithful and just to forgive us our sins and to cleanse us from all wickedness." (1 John 1:9)

God has very good plans for us. "For I know the plans I have for you," says the LORD. "They are plans for good and not for disaster, to give you a future and a hope." (Jeremiah 29:11)

Still, it's good to set short, medium, and long-term life goals. Set goals in the important areas of life; spiritual, physical, financial, work/career, children, and education. Under each goal list the steps you need to take to achieve that goal. Most importantly, pray before you put the pen to paper and afterwards pray, "not my will but Thine be done." Proceed to let God guide your steps. These are godly plans.

You will be amazed when you review your goals a year later and realize you've accomplished more than you ever thought possible. As it says in Ephesians 3:20; "Now all glory to God, who is able, through his mighty power at work within us, to accomplish infinitely more than we might ask or think."

Recall in Proverbs 3:5-6 we are reminded that we are not to lean on our own understanding. Our life plans are limited. When we keep our heart and mind on God, His plans become our plans. We find our will has aligned with God's will for us. This is what it means when it says in Psalm 37:4, "Take delight in the LORD, and he will give you your heart's desires."

Moving on to another practical subject, Proverbs 12:10 speaks to us animal lovers: "The godly care for their animals, but the wicked are always cruel."

It's important to take responsibility for animals in our care. If we can't take care of their needs, we need to ensure they receive new owners who can.

It's wise to spay and neuter cats and dogs, as well as provide medical maintenance to all animals. If our pets are overweight, it's likely due to unhealthy food. Good pet food costs more money than the cheap stuff and good, quality food is far healthier for our animals' lives and quality of life. Cruelty includes not providing time and attention to our domesticated pets. These guys want our love!

When quality of life is poor due to chronic sickness an animal may need to be put down. If an animal we own is in pain, very old, and miserable, we are being selfish and cruel to keep it alive. People put an undue amount of emotion into relationships with pets; sometimes to a point of worship. The Bible puts far more importance on many other things. Yes, we love them but they are not people.

Our animal friends bring us joy, companionship, and sustenance. They are dependent on us to ensure they are well cared for. When we take care of our animals, we demonstrate wisdom, good judgment, and good stewardship. This includes discipline and training where necessary, and involves keeping them safe and contained as well. A "free-range" Labrador in the cul-de-sac is not wise or responsible.

If an animal seriously harms another animal or person, it needs to be dealt with in an appropriate manner that prevents the harm from ever happening again. Sometimes that means putting the animal to death. That is super sad and not what you would hope for, so do everything possible to train them and keep them out of trouble.

We have a responsibility, given by God, to be good stewards of our pets, livestock as well as all animals in creation; "Then God said, "Let us make mankind in our image, in our likeness, so that they may rule over the fish in the sea and the birds in the sky, over the livestock and all the wild animals, and over all the creatures that move along the ground" Genesis 1:26.

We've talked about the value of serving. If you have a great love for animals, there are numerous serving opportunities in the community where you can care for pets that need it.

Wisdom is not rocket science but it is practical.

Proverbs 13 – GETTING AND GIVING CORRECTION

Read Proverbs 13.

Most people do not like to receive discipline. To be corrected or chastised hits us straight in the pride. It hurts and it's embarrassing! Verse 1 says accepting discipline is wise and Verse 13 and 18 say to accept correction and be successful and honored.

This is very difficult for those of us who are thin-skinned.

Proverbs is talking about correction and discipline that is for our good. Usually, it's described as father to a son. As we build good judgment, we'll be able to better discern when the correction is wise and from God. It will usually come from other people, so it's very important to have trustworthy and wise people in your life.

There are always people in life who are critical in a hurtful way. Verbal abuse and degrading words are never okay and they do not come from God. As we grow in wisdom and discernment, these people have less and less power to hurt us. We also lose interest in spending time with people who are abusive. If you're in a verbally abusive relationship, find someone you can trust to confide in. If it's a verbally abusive situation at work, deal with it directly through your Human Resources Department and/or start looking hard for a new job. God will guide you and protect you in these things.

Here we're talking about areas where God wants to change us to ultimately make us happier. Do you see the difference between kids whose parents discipline them versus kids who have no discipline? Kids who receive healthy discipline are happy and well-adjusted. (That's another chapter!) We're God's kids.

We may have to receive correction from someone who has power over us, such as a boss or law enforcement. How we react and how we process it is where wisdom comes in. To refuse the discipline is another option. We can rebel, resist, and react in anger or defensiveness. No matter who is delivering the correction, these are rarely wise reactions.

A key factor in this issue is pride. Pride comes before a fall and often ends in humiliation. Verse 18 uses an example where pride results in poverty and disgrace. No matter how devastated we feel inside at a valid criticism (and the valid ones usually hurt the worst) we need to accept it. God is very patient with us, but it's probably something in us that needs to change. If we accept it well, the end result is honor and wisdom, and we are changed.

What is the wise way to receive correction and discipline? Don't instantly react negatively and defensively denying the criticism. You can say words like, "Thank-you for telling me this. Of course, I don't like it and I need to think about it before I punch you, (just kidding on that last part). I'd like to respond after I've had time." If it's appropriate, you may come back with a plan showing steps you are going to take to make changes. This is the kind of response that is suitable for work or some type of professional situation, (obviously not the punching part).

If the correction is within a more intimate relationship, you can grit your teeth and say something similar to, "I don't like hearing this but I appreciate you being honest with me." You may engage in deeper conversation at that point. Just be aware that your feelings are hurt and if you need to, ask for time before responding.

Overall, a humble response is the way to receive discipline or correction. Easier said than done. If necessary go in the bathroom, look in the mirror and repeat 77 times, "I can do everything through Christ, who gives me strength." (Philippians 4:13)

Seriously, after receiving the correction, find someplace to be alone and pray. Always face it head on. Ask God for wisdom and comfort. If it's something where you need to ask for forgiveness then do so. Ask God to change you.

One of the most powerful prayers we can pray when we are angry and hurt is to ask God to keep our hearts soft. Many of us want to harden our hearts and shut down. We all want to protect our pride when the truth is, we need to destroy it. This is an opportunity to do that. Ask God to take away our ego and pride.

Wisdom requires a soft heart, thick skin, and a willingness to be vulnerable. It's also powerful to thank God for this opportunity to change, and to thank Him for the discipline. This is especially true in marriage relationships where keeping our hearts soft is crucial to the survival of our marriage.

Proverbs also provides guidance on how to give correction and discipline. We want the person to receive it well so they can grow in wisdom. This isn't easy either! It's important to look at our motives when we're criticizing someone – especially those closest to us. Verse 17 says a reliable messenger brings healing.

Heartfelt and thoughtful correction is a good thing that comes from God, and should be given and received prayerfully.

One common method that seems to help is the "sandwich" method; give positive input, then the correction, and then more positive input. In intimate relationships, be sure to include a lot of love. Ideally, the person walks away happy to have received the discipline! The best leaders are those who do a good job of discipline.

If you are a critical person in general then it is wise to guard your tongue. Chances are, your critical attitude has been an issue in every relationship you've had with the opposite sex. You want to change people. If you have kids, they are impacted by it. You have a mindset of "it's never good enough" and it typically comes from a perfectionist personality. It's almost impossible to accept others for who they are – especially those closest to us. People like this are very hard on themselves too. It is not healthy and it's destructive to relationships. It creates insecurity in others.

It's time to stop this behavior.

How do you stop being negatively critical? First, repent. Admit that there's a problem and ask God to change you. These types of character flaws are usually deep-seated and we need God to make these changes. There's a saying "you can't fix a broken tool with a broken tool." We need a God who is bigger than us in order to change. Next, talk to someone you trust, and confide in them this area of struggle. Tell them you want to change. Maybe it's appropriate for you to apologize to those you love. Be willing to change. If you're not quite willing, then be willing to be willing.

It starts in our head and usually ends up coming out of our mouth. It's absolutely necessary for us to change critical thinking, even for people we don't like much and especially people we love. Don't talk about people behind their backs in this way, especially your spouse. Just stop. In fact, purposely mention positive things about him/her out loud to other people. We need to catch those negative thoughts and replace them with positive aspects of the person we are tearing down in our mind.

Overall, for all scenarios described here, it boils down to a humble response. When we get humble before a God who knows every single thing about us and are willing to change. He will do miracles.

Proverbs 14 – YOUR INSIDES ARE SHOWING

Read Proverbs 14.

Whatever is on the inside of us shows on the outside. Our actions, lifestyle practices, and outward behaviors tell the story of what is in our heart.

In Verse 18 it says simpletons are clothed with foolishness, but the prudent are crowned with knowledge. Just as Verse 24 says wealth is a crown for the wise.

In both of the above verses, there is reference to a crown. What is a crown? It's typically a symbol of royalty, honor, leadership, and prestige. It's also associated with beauty and treasure. What an awesome thing to have showing!

Prudence, wisdom, discernment, and good judgment are only possible if we fear God. As we have learned throughout Proverbs, a healthy fear of God comes when we know that we are tiny and He is huge. Humility requires that we purposely spend quiet time to get back to tiny. Too often we naturally start to, "drift away from the dock" toward ego. It's a constant battle. An intimate prayer life is key. Humility is foundational to wisdom. It would seem we can't be crowned if we are prideful.

God, the King of Kings, the supreme and almighty royal Lord of Heaven, sent His only son to earth to wear a crown of thorns. If humility is the source of true wisdom, then there is a lot of false wisdom in the world. Make no mistake; you are embarking on a path that is not compatible with this world's value systems!

Verse 33 says, "Wisdom is enshrined in an understanding heart." We understand God places the highest value on humility. We understand wisdom was with God for all eternity and is His delight. We understand God loves wisdom. With this understanding, wisdom is protected and preserved in our heart. It is enshrined because we adore wisdom. Think of shrines where there are mementos, images, and remembrances. They are places of reverence and respect. This describes the incredible value we place on wisdom enshrined within our heart in Verse 33.

Right along with God's love of humility is Proverbs' consistent instruction to help the poor. These are outside acts that reflect the inner heart.

Blessed are those who help the poor. (Verse 21) If you plan to do good, you will receive unfailing love and faithfulness. (Verse 22) Think about that. Is there any human being or entity who can really provide unfailing love and faithfulness? Unfailing is the key word here. We know that only God can truly provide unfailing love and faithfulness, so this is a direct promise from Him. Verse 31 says helping the poor honors God.

We can always find others who are needy, and take that step of faith to give even a little bit. To do this consistently will result in blessings from God.

It's safe to say that God does not guarantee we will get rich with money, but he promises crowns and treasures.   It's also a practical truth that when we are wise we make better choices with money, and are able to build wealth, and are then able to give more. If we are faithfully giving, God will provide more for us to give.

Hard work brings profit. (Verse 23)   Once again, our actions (hard work) and their results (profit) are outer reflections of our inner life. Another way this rich life of wisdom shows on the outside is in a peaceful heart that leads to a healthy body. (Verse 30)

Emotional pain and upheaval show up on the outside and are usually associated with a life of foolishness.   In fact, the second part of Verse 30 says, "…jealousy is like cancer in the bones." If you've ever experienced the emotion of jealousy, you know it feels sick and unhealthy. It is nothing that comes from God and is rooted in deep-seated insecurity.

If we are lacking peace in our hearts the best way to get there is to seek God.   Seek His face and His will, and find that nugget of wisdom in whatever situation we're in. Sometimes it's an action we need to take or amends to make. Maybe we need to get a hug, or give a hug. Often the best thing to do is get out of our selves.

Don't underestimate the immediate comfort that comes from picking up your Bible during stressful times. Better yet, have the Word planted in your heart with special verses you've memorized. You'll be tapping into supernatural power and help.

Jesus said in John 14:27, "I am leaving you with a gift--peace of mind and heart. And the peace I give is a gift the world cannot give. So don't be troubled or afraid." He is called the Prince of Peace. In John 1:1 it says that the Word has been with God from the beginning. Then in John 1:14 it says the Word became flesh. Jesus is the Word. Jesus, peace, and wisdom are ours to have.

The power of God's Word (Jesus) planted supernaturally in our heart and mind impacts all areas of life, including our physical health. Stress has been proven to make us physically sick. Conversely, peace and joy prolong life making it rich and satisfying. Let's repeat Verse 30(a), "A peaceful heart leads to a healthy body."

We find as we grow in spiritual maturity and continue to acquire wisdom, we have a low tolerance for peace-killers like guilt. To be clear, guilt is not bad. Verse 9 says, "Fools make fun of guilt, but the godly acknowledge it and seek reconciliation." There are voices in this world that claim guilt is bad and should be banished from our lives. That's simply not true. Guilt is good as long as we quickly seek to resolve it.

If we feel guilty about something it's time to make a change. Hopefully it's uncomfortable and painful enough to motivate us! For instance, if we feel guilty for gossiping, maybe next time we're tempted to do so we'll remember the discomfort and turn away from it. With that change comes peace in our heart.

There is real danger in ignoring guilt and hardening our hearts. Guilt that is not reconciled turns to shame. Shame is when we are trying to hide ourselves from God, and it is definitely not good. Don't get guilt and shame confused.

Living a life of wisdom is not complicated and it's not always easy, but the rewards are beyond measure. It shows on the outside for others to see. As we continue to build wisdom into our lives with consistent practice, people will notice something in you. Although the crown you wear may be invisible, it shows.

Proverbs 15 – WHY DOES GOD ALLOW EVIL?

Read Proverbs 15.

"The Lord is watching everywhere; keeping His eye on both the evil and the good" Proverbs 15:3.

Warning – this chapter is another deep one. You can handle it!

God is omniscient, omnipresent and omnipotent: all-knowing, present everywhere at all times and all-powerful. There is no being who comes close to God's power. We barely understand it.

Many of us often wonder how God can allow so much evil in the world when He's supposed to be all-powerful. When we hear of horror and abuse of the innocent, it seems like He's distant and uninvolved. If God is watching everywhere, keeping His eye on both the evil and the good, why does He let these senseless acts of evil happen?

One thing is, we need to accept that His thoughts are not our thoughts, and our ways are not His ways as it says in Isaiah 55:8. It's important to get this. We want to make God manageable in our limited understanding. We want Him to comply with our will of how we think things should be. In other words, He should not allow the revolting evil that takes place in this world.

He knows every tragedy and heartbreak, and he counts up every tear. Psalm 56:8 says, "You keep track of all my sorrows. You have collected all my tears in your bottle. You have recorded each one in your book."

He is intimately involved in every detail of your life. He knows every hair on your head (Matthew 10:30) and He knows every thought and move you make (Psalm 139:3). These are all verses well worth reading and studying.

Yes, He knows every tragedy and heartbreak. In fact, He's right there in the midst of it, suffering with the hurting people He loves so much. The real question is, how does he bear it? We are deeply disturbed by a headline but He is intimately involved with the situation. Can you imagine knowing every single tragedy that has taken place? Not to mention knowing ones that are yet to happen?

Evil is a direct result of free will. God could stop all evil. God could also force all people to obey Him. During this life we all have free choice. Let's be clear here. God is one hundred percent good. There is no darkness in Him only light. Evil is from Satan. There is no light in Satan. The evil in the world comes from evil forces. Ephesians 6:12 says, "For we are not fighting against flesh-and-blood enemies, but against evil rulers and authorities of the unseen world, against mighty powers in this dark world, and against evil spirits in the heavenly places."

We still haven't answered the original question; why does it seem like God has let Satan win the battle? He hasn't! Satan has already lost the war. When Jesus rose from the grave, He defeated sin and death. God is allowing free will so as many people as possible can be saved through Jesus Christ.

There's a reason why humans instinctively love and prefer happy endings. It's how our Creator made us. There is a gloriously happy ending.

Revelations 21:3-4 says, "I heard a loud shout from the throne, saying, "Look, God's home is now among His people! He will live with them, and they will be his people. God, Himself will be with them. He will wipe every tear from their eyes, and there will be no more death or sorrow or crying or pain. All these things are gone forever."

God is a just God and there will be justice one day. Google 'God's justice in the Bible' sometime.

With regard to this world's trouble, 2 Peter 3:8-9 says, "But you must not forget this one thing, dear friends: A day is like a thousand years to the Lord, and a thousand years is like a day. The Lord isn't really being slow about his promise, as some people think. No, he is being patient for your sake. He does not want anyone to be destroyed, but wants everyone to repent." He is allowing free will.

During this life we all get to choose which path we take. This choice has eternal implications. God could force us to obey Him. Easily. He passionately desires for us to choose to love Him. Christianity is the only faith in the world that entails God pursuing man. All other religions are man pursuing God. It's also the only faith where the foundation is based on an intimate relationship with God.

Those of us blessed to know God are to be a light in the darkness, and trust that He knows what He's doing. More importantly, we need to know there is absolutely nothing hidden from God. There are no dark places of secrecy. Stop and think about that. There is nothing hidden from God, neither good nor evil. There are no secrets. He knows the human heart. (Verse 11)

He knows everything about you. Now also consider that he loves and adores you. His prime desire is a relationship with you. Verses 9 and 29 tell us He delights and hears the prayers of the upright, (that would be us). This is a truth that is worth meditating on. It will bring a deeper security and acceptance to our lives, and allow us to bring light to others in this dark world. The God of the universe delights in our prayers. That is a motivator!

Proverbs tells us over and again that God detests evil. He knows the plans of the evil ones and there is nothing hidden from Him. The Bible says one day there will be justice.

Accept there are some things in this life we won't understand when it comes to God. In the meantime, willfully allow Him into every deep, dark, hidden place inside. Let's concern ourselves more with the things that we do understand about God, based on His Word.

Proverbs 16 – HOW TO BE SUCCESSFUL AT WORK

Read Proverbs 16.

Living a life of graciousness, wisdom, and right actions can benefit us politically, and raise us to powerful and influential positions. Leadership is a gift and a spiritual responsibility.

Genuinely honest and good individuals are attractive, and other people place trust in them. This is true strength. The epitome of this kind of strength is Jesus. He attracted huge crowds of people and they dropped everything in their lives to follow Him. He was the ultimate force for good.

This strength does not back down from the truth even in the face of death itself. Amazingly, we have this strength inside of us!

Jesus was the perfect example of the quality of humility we've been talking about. When we combine humility and strength, we are able to persuade and influence others. With wisdom we are able to be highly effective and achieve results. We are trustworthy.

When we prove our integrity by our actions, people will look to us for leadership. We gain respect and esteem in the eyes of others when we boldly stand upon our integrity.

The first chapter in the book of Daniel is an excellent example of this type of power and prestige. Daniel stands upon his faith and his value systems, and is quickly elevated to a position of power. Jacob's son Joseph is another example of a person of godliness and integrity leading to a very powerful position. He went from being a slave to ruling all of Egypt second only to the Pharaoh.

The king is pleased with words from righteous lips; he loves those who speak honestly. (Verse 13) Both Daniel and Joseph spoke honestly from a place of righteousness with God. They were wise because of their right relationship with God and achieved amazing results in their work that impressed their leaders. Proverbs 16:7 makes the meaningful statement that when our lives please the Lord, even our enemies are at peace with us.

We will succeed at work if we use discretion and good judgment along with honesty. Even in a highly political environment where it would seem only "brown-nosers" prevail, we need to remember we live to please God, not man. It takes a lot of pressure off.

It's important to remember the words in Verse 3 which say, "Commit your actions to the Lord and your plans will succeed." Maybe you do have ambitions to advance your career or position within some organization. It's vital that you don't allow pride and selfish ambition to undermine the strength and power that God honors. As we've seen consistently in Proverbs, and throughout chapter 16, we need to ensure we are aligned with God's will, which is always to be humble. This is not easy and requires a lot of prayer!

Jesus lowered Himself from a position, literally as one with God in heaven. He came to Earth to lead people. See Philippians 2:6-8. If you have the time, go read these verses now. They're the perfect Scriptures about humility.

If you have the gift of leadership, it is a gift from God. Influence, power and leadership are gifts that we need to submit to God for His purposes. Servant leadership is an incredibly important topic that will be studied more fully at another time. As it is, humility is the foundation of servant leadership and the heart of Jesus. He emptied Himself for us and He was the greatest leader who ever lived. Millions follow Him to this day.

As we grow in good judgment and humility we will use words wisely. Our work ethic is without question and we show discretion. We are attractive and persuasive in a way that stands out because we have the power of wisdom dwelling in us. Verse 21 says the wise are known for their understanding, and pleasant words are persuasive. Just as Verse 23 says from a wise mind comes wise speech; the words of the wise are persuasive. It appears God really wanted us to get that message about persuasiveness! Hmmmm.

Verse 32 shows us real influence and strength; "better to be patient than powerful; better to have self-control than conquer a city." A life of wisdom provides a power that goes far beyond position. We have the power of influence and God can use that.

Let's be clear, position is not required to be a great leader. You can be the lowliest mailroom clerk and have great influence and strength with your fellow men.

We've determined that our value system and the world's value system are not the same. That doesn't mean we can't shine in this world. In fact, just the opposite is true. We are called to be a light in the darkness. Daniel, Joseph, David, Moses and many other wildly successful biblical leaders and achievers have one thing in common; their worldly success was directly tied to them submitting everything to God.

God wants to use you at work and at any other organization where you have the ability influence others and to be an example. If you're in a position of power, then let God use you for His purposes.

Proverbs 17 – THE VALUE OF LISTENING

Read Proverbs 17.

In Proverbs 17 we find verse 28 which provides a little peek into God's sense of humor; "Even a fool is thought wise when he is silent. With their mouth shut they seem intelligent." The irony is that very rarely in Proverbs do fools keep silent. In fact, jumping ahead to Proverbs 18 you'll see in Verse 2 it says, "A fool takes no pleasure in understanding, but only in expressing his opinion."

Do your words get you in trouble? So often in conversations and situations you see multiple people vying to be heard. You see it on TV opinion shows where everybody is talking at the same time, speaking louder and louder, because their opinion is "right." It's even in the workplace during meetings where interruptions are a normal part of discourse. People are pushing their viewpoints trying to be heard above others. It happens in the backseat of cars anytime you have more than one kid, and the noise level continues to escalate.

It's a very loud world and there is a lot of competition to be heard. Do you feel like if you don't speak out you will get trampled over and left in the dust? In the midst of the clamor, how do we follow Verse 27 and conduct ourselves as a truly wise person who uses few words?

Sensible people keep their eyes glued on wisdom. (Verse 24a) As we have read in Proverbs, it is wise to think things through. Is what I think I need to say really all that important? Is it crucial to express my opinion? When we seek to be humble, that highly attractive quality, we are better able to listen and observe. We also have the inner quietness to stop and assess our motives.

The key is listening and when we do speak, ideally it's to add value and wisdom to the conversation. Psalm 19:14 perfectly sums up this intention; "May the words of my lips and the meditations of my heart be pleasing to you my Lord, my rock and my redeemer." This is a great memory verse for life.

Remember as wisdom seekers we value knowledge, understanding, and discernment. So far we haven't read anything in Proverbs where expressing our opinion is all that important. Those of us who are very opinionated probably need to do some soul-searching about how this relates to our pride. It's hard when we are so darn right!

Being a good listener is a trait that is compatible with wisdom. This trait will help all relationships! In his book *The 7 Habits of Highly Effective People* Stephen Covey teaches to seek first to understand, then to be understood. You'll find when you ask questions people magically pay attention to you. When you ask probing questions it persuades people to look at things from a different perspective. It's time to set our opinion aside for a minute and be curious.

Think of a situation where you have vast difference of opinion with someone. Let's say politics. Can you imagine trying to truly understand where the other person is coming from? Instead of arguing, continue to ask questions. Then ask even more questions. It doesn't mean you have to agree with them, but ultimately it will provide opportunity for a more meaningful dialog. Maybe you are having a conversation with someone who hates God. Wouldn't it be important to truly understand why they are where they're at? Next time you and your spouse or friend are in a heated argument, stop and seek to understand. You might be amazed at the change in the conversation.

Be curious about other's viewpoints and opinions and you'll find people will be drawn to you, and you'll be able to connect with them in a new way. This is a habit that takes practice to develop. Thankfully, we have opportunities everyday to try to apply this new skill.

In a work situation we can take notes as we listen and try to better understand. Sometimes we are afraid to ask questions because we think we'll look foolish. You'd be surprised to find that so often other people in the room have the same questions! Don't be afraid to ask.

As a side note, in today's online media, people rampantly spout their opinions. They can do it anonymously which has removed all restraint. It's not wise and in some cases is actually evil and harmful.

It's pure self-gratification and provides a stark example of Proverbs 18:2. There is no seeking to understand. It is a good practice to immediately desist in participating in this meaningless use of time.

On the other hand, online communities are a reality of our society. Commit to providing meaningful content on social media and keep all exchanges positive. Imagine Jesus is reading everything you write...because He is.

Ultimately, we need to place a much higher value on face-to-face relationships and practice listening skills while participating in "icontact." This might be a good time to text a friend and make the effort to set up some time to get together. It's so much more satisfying to our souls.

To hold the tongue takes practice and a lot of prayer. It doesn't come naturally in our culture. There are opportunities to practice every day, and today is the day to start!

Proverbs 18 – HOW TO FEEL SAFE AND SECURE IN THE STORM

Read Proverbs 18.

Verse 18: "The name of the Lord is a strong fortress, the godly run to Him and are safe." This verse could bring to mind an image of running to some place safe as if we are running away in fear. A much better perspective is running in pursuit of God. Instead of running away from something, we are chasing after it.

It's important to note that He pursued us first. We pursue God because we love Him, not because it's required in order to be accepted by Him. We pursue Him only because He pursued us first.

We chase a lot of things in life. We chase our dreams, we chase after wealth, love, and satisfaction. It seems as though we are constantly striving in this life. It's like we were made that way. Well, isn't that interesting? What do you pursue with passion or even obsession? Have you ever been consumed with a purpose? We were made for purpose.

For most of us it doesn't come naturally to pursue God. It's an act of will. Purpose and passion is cultivated over a lifetime of discipline and creating habits of devotion. It takes work! Do you still pursue your spouse with the same passion as when you were dating? Maybe not, but on the other hand, hopefully we are pursuing healthy marriages and relationships. We find this pursuit requires a willful act versus an emotionally driven or obsessive act.

Daily time with the Bible, and the simple act of seeking Him in our everyday lives, creates the right momentum. Next thing we know, we start to experience a deep-seated, unshakeable security. It takes time for us to gain even a sliver of understanding of God's passionate love for us. It happens when we study His Word. It's why He has given it to us. Reading the Bible and prayer are how we pursue His presence. After a while, we find it becomes like nourishment and we feel empty without it. This is how we are changed from the inside out.

We know no matter what happens, God is with us and will never leave us. He has shown this over and over again in our lives and in His Word.

The Bible says in Deuteronomy 31:6, "So be strong and courageous! Do not be afraid and do not panic before them. For the LORD your God will personally go ahead of you. He will neither fail you nor abandon you." He means never. This also means he's already been where you're going. God is way beyond what we understand about time. He knows your future and He's got your back.

Throughout the Bible are promises of his protection, guidance, and provision. We rest with a security that is like a strong fortress which can withstand the battering of life's storms. Imagine a brutal battle going on and you're safe within an impenetrable fortress with nothing to fear.

When we start relying on wealth, other people, or material stuff, our security will slip. These things can crumble and storms of life can destroy them. Verse 11 says, "The rich think of their wealth as a strong defense; they imagine it to be a high wall of safety." This is false security and it relies on things that can be taken away. Stock markets crash, jobs are lost, businesses fail, illnesses and death are all a part of this life.

On the other hand, Romans 8:38-39 says, "And I am convinced that nothing can ever separate us from God's love. Neither death nor life, neither angels nor demons, neither our fears for today, nor our worries about tomorrow—not even the powers of hell can separate us from God's love. No power in the sky above or in the earth below—indeed, nothing in all creation will ever be able to separate us from the love of God who is revealed in Christ Jesus our Lord."

Now let's remember there is nothing more powerful than God and He loves us with an overwhelming passion. (Go back and read Psalm 139 again) No one or nothing can ever take that away.

God will meet all of our needs just as a good parent meets their child's needs. In Matthew 10:29-31 Jesus gave us these reassuring words, "What is the price of two sparrows—one copper coin? But not a single sparrow can fall to the ground without your Father knowing it. And the very hairs on your head are all numbered. So don't be afraid; you are more valuable to God than a whole flock of sparrows." It's extremely important that we understand this and let it penetrate supernaturally into our hearts and minds. It is the key to true security.

Nowhere in the Bible does it say we won't experience hardship in life. It does say we can experience peace and joy in spite of life's circumstances. The alternative is to place our security in things that we know, deep inside, are not eternal and can be taken. This leads to insecurity and fear.

It boils down to evaluating what we cling to most tightly. When you thank God, what are the first things you're most grateful for? This will reflect what you value the most. Gratitude is an excellent habit. Let's first thank God for His love for us and for His Word. When the Word is planted in your heart, nobody can ever take that away. Through the Word, His wisdom lives inside us along with knowledge of His obsessive love. These are eternal gifts that can never be taken away. This anchors our security.

Maybe the best we can do at this point is agree with Psalm 139:6, "such knowledge is too wonderful for me, too great for me to understand!" It's all good.

It's important to pray and to purposely nurture your relationship with God. Pour your heart out to Him. Thank Him for His gracious and unconditional love every day.

Let's pursue God with purpose on purpose. When we start to live a life with the security that comes with clinging to the eternal, we get to share this security with others. So many people are living in fear in the world because they are putting their faith in the things that won't last. We are a light in the darkness.

Proverbs 19 – HOW TO GIVE TO THE POOR

Read Proverbs 19.

One of the distinctions of God's wisdom is the consistent command to help the poor. In our society there are plenty of opportunities to help. Also, unfortunately, in our society there is some confusion about how to help the poor.

There are organizations that you can give to that are supposed to funnel the money you give to the poor. There are no guarantees it will go where you had intended. A local church you belong to, where you are confident in their money management, is usually a good option. Many times you can give to a "benevolent fund" at church. This is used to help those in financial need. A solid church will be transparent with finances and provide transparency on all inputs and outputs of the money donated.

If you are in true financial need and belong to a church, talk openly to your pastor. Sometimes they can help with a car payment, medical bills, or groceries. Food is abundantly available at food banks and food closets that are run by churches. Contact local churches and ask about resources. What you'll find is a sincere desire to help. You will get the opportunity to experience God's love and compassion for the poor. At the same time, pray with faith to a God who knows all of your needs and promises to care for you.

Sometimes we see people standing on street corners holding up signs. When it's a young healthy person, wisdom tells us this is not a good place to put our money. There are many of these people who probably fit the profiles in Verses 15 and 24; Idleness leaves them hungry. They are somewhat humorously described as being too lazy to even lift food to their mouth. These are people, for whatever reason, who refuse to put the effort into being self-sufficient. God promises He'll meet all our needs, but wisdom requires we must put in the effort to do our part.

In our society, anybody can find help through local missions, shelters, and churches. Giving to these organizations is a sound way to ensure your giving is directed to meet the needs of the poor. We need to be wise where we give.

The intent of the Scripture is practical. It's a way to spread wealth that is not based on a political ideology or dependent upon government. If everybody gave generously from the heart, there would be less of a need for government assistance.

More importantly, it's a spiritual issue. When we include giving as part of our monthly budget it alters our viewpoint of money. This is particularly true if we give to the poor in the name of the Lord and do it out of obedience. As Verse 17 says, we are giving to the Lord and will be repaid. (Make note, charitable giving is above tithes and offerings.) When we are obedient to that tug on our hearts to give, we are acting on faith and it helps take away our financial fears. It also reminds us that we have a God of abundance, not of lack.

Even if you don't think you can afford to give, do it anyway. Give $5 a month in the name of the Lord with gratitude to Him. Your act of faith will be rewarded – that's a promise from the Word of God.

Here's is one of the many things Jesus said about giving to the poor, "And He sat down opposite the treasury, and began observing how the people were putting money into the treasury; and many rich people were putting in large sums. A poor widow came and put in two small copper coins, which amount to a cent. Calling His disciples to Him, He said to them, 'Truly I say to you, this poor widow put in more than all the contributors to the treasury; for they all put in out of their surplus, but she, out of her poverty, put in all she owned, all she had to live on.'"

Surely He was pleased with the large amounts given by the wealthy folks, but He was exceedingly impressed with the poor widow. She displayed faith with her giving. Another thing we can be sure of is He is very much aware, and observing everything we give.

With a perspective of abundance we are free to give because we know we are being provided for. If we think God won't provide, we hoard our money in fear. An excellent example of God's abundance is in Matthew 14:15-21 where Jesus fed 5000 people with five loaves of bread and two fish. There were leftovers. That is abundance! Don't ever doubt God's provision for you. In the Lord's

87

Prayer when we say, "give us this day our daily bread", this is simply asking for God to provide our needs. As a note, the Lord's Prayer was specifically given by Jesus for us to pray in Matthew 6:9. He gave this prayer right after He gave instruction about giving to the poor in Matthew 6:3.

As wisdom grows in our hearts, so will our generosity. We will feel conviction to give out of gratitude, and even obligation. God wants to meet the needs of the poor through us. The more we give, the more He will give to us so we can give more. We will reflect His abundance. You cannot "out give" God. Poverty does not come from God. If everybody gave as He intends, poverty would be abolished.

Proverbs 20 – HOW TO BE JUSTIFIED

Read Proverbs 20.

The good news is God is a God of true justice; right and wrong. There is not a gray area with God. Verse 10 says, "False weights and unequal measures – the Lord detests double standards of all kind."

The concept of moral relativism says whatever is right for you is right, and whatever is wrong for you is wrong. In other words, there is no absolute morality. This concept is not from God. God is perfectly holy, purely good, and perfectly just. In fact, just as darkness can't abide in light (think about that), evil cannot survive in God's presence. In 1 John 1:5 it says, "This is the message we heard from Jesus and now declare to you: God is light, and there is no darkness in him at all."

The bad news is God is a God of true justice. We are not good enough to be in His presence. Verse 9 asks, "who can say 'I have cleansed my heart, I am pure and free from sin?'" We all fall short. None of us can be perfectly holy. Think of the Ten Commandments. (Exodus 20:1-24) None of us can honestly say we have never broken one of these commands from God. Not Mother Theresa or the most decent, giving, honest, and good person you know. God's standard is perfection and there is no compromise. Are you feeling the pressure yet?

All religions besides Christianity are performance-based on being good enough to get to heaven. There are certain acts that need to be performed, ways to dress, ways to serve, pray, eat, and other parameters. This is called legalism. Oh yes, there are Christians who fall into this lie too.

Sorry, we cannot purify ourselves and there is nothing we can do to be good enough to be right with God. That is why God provides a way for us to be purified. That is the real good news. It is through Jesus Christ. That is the foundational basis of the Bible. In fact, Jesus tells us this Himself. John 4:6 says, "Jesus told him, 'I am the way, the truth, and the life. No one can come to the Father except through me'". Most people recognize John 3:16; "For God so loved the world that he gave his one and only Son, that whoever believes in him shall not perish but have eternal life." (NIV) It's important to read Verse 17 as well which says, "For God did not send his Son into the world to condemn the world, but to save the world through him." (NIV)

If you are not a believer but want to know more, read Romans 10:9-10 for direction. The first step is to believe you fall short of God's perfection. The next step is desire to be right with God. Surely you have a Christian friend you can talk to.

If God is just, why is there so much evil in this world? Why does He allow it? Well, the other good news is that He is patient. One primary reason evil is present is due to free will. God could easily eradicate all evil from His creation, but that would also eradicate those who have not accepted the purifying salvation of Jesus Christ. He is not willing that any should perish and that all should find Him. (2 Peter 3:9)

A better question to ask is, how does He bear it? There is nothing hidden from God. He is very much aware of every one of the atrocities and abuses that have ever happened and that are taking place at this moment. Verse 27 says the Lord's light penetrates the human spirit, exposing every hidden motive. He knows about the evil before it happens. Think of how we feel when we hear about the abuse of innocents. We are heartbroken, horrified, and disturbed. Imagine how God, the creator of emotions, must feel. He is with the victims and the hurting. Jesus Christ was the ultimate innocent. He was one hundred percent without sin, falsely accused, and imprisoned. He was physically beaten nearly to death, publicly humiliated, and ultimately executed in a horrific and painful manner. This was God's beloved son. He feels our pain and grieves with us in our tragedies.

In the end, the good news is God is a God of justice. There will be justice and evil will ultimately be eradicated. One of Jesus' last statements as He drew his last breath on the cross was, "it is finished" (John 19:30). Evil was defeated when Jesus rose from the grave in victory. Until he comes back to exterminate evil once and for all, we continue to be hope and light in the darkness while there's still time.

There will come a time where God's light will rule earth where darkness (injustice) will no longer be able to exist. These are scriptural truths in both the Old Testament and the New Testament that are worth digging into with a study Bible. Below are just a few of the many verses that talk about His eventual reign here on Earth:

Psalm 2:6-9, Psalm 22:27-31, Psalm 47, Psalm 67, Isaiah 2:1-4, Isaiah 9:6-7, Isaiah 11:3b-9, Isaiah 24:21-23, 2 Thessalonians 1:7-10, 2 Timothy 2:12, Revelations 12:5, Revelations 19:15-16, and Luke 1:26-38.

If you have not accepted Jesus as your personal savior, then at least be willing to be willing. You've made it this far in your quest for a life of wisdom; you've honestly got nothing to lose.

If you are a believer, rejoice that He paid the price for your sins and you are justified before a just God!

Proverbs 21 – HOW TO HAVE FINANCIAL SECURITY

Read Proverbs 21.

Proverbs has a lot to say about wealth and prosperity. It's easy to derive from these Scriptures that God will make us rich. Unfortunately, there are many preachers who use this as a way to draw people in with promises of wealth and prosperity. It is called the "prosperity gospel". It ignores the very important truth that wealth and prosperity in God's eyes are much different than worldly wealth and prosperity.

God's will for us, above all else, is a rich and satisfying life that is blessed by peace, harmony, and a deep-seated security that can never be shaken. He also says it's very hard to be money-rich and have that peace. We so easily shift our security away from a spiritually stable foundation to one of material wealth.

Jesus, in His infinite wisdom said this about riches, "Don't store up treasures here on earth, where moths eat them and rust destroys them, and where thieves break in and steal. Store your treasures in heaven, where moths and rust cannot destroy, and thieves do not break in and steal. Wherever your treasure is, there the desires of your heart will also be." (Matthew 6:19-21)

Nowhere in Scripture does God say we must be in poverty in order to be holy, wise, or godly. In fact Proverbs 30:8-9 says that being too poor is not good anymore than being too rich. Proverbs 20:17-20 provides even more insight. Verse 17 says, "those who love pleasure become poor; those who love wine and luxury will never be rich." The key word here is "love." Whereas Verse 20 does say, "the wise have wealth and luxury, but fools spend whatever they get." Most of us can appreciate wealth and luxury! The wise described here are obviously those who are wise with their finances.

We remember from chapter 1, the wise are those who fear God. The wise are humble and they give generously, "The godly love to give." (Verse 26) They have an excellent work ethic and enjoy a sterling reputation. The wise understand the value of spiritual treasures far above worldly treasures. We are deeply secure that God will faithfully meet all of our needs and we cling very loosely to the things of this world.

God specifically blessed many people in the Bible with vast amounts of wealth and treasure. You can be sure that those so blessed strived to place God above their material wealth. He also stripped kingdoms away from fools. Read 1 and 2 Kings to see numerous examples of this.

When we are wise, we work hard to get out and stay out of debt, we save for emergencies, we tithe, and we give to the poor. We trust God. These practical acts of wisdom allow us to build wealth while keeping the right perspective on money. We have a deep-seated security that prevails through the changing winds of fortune.

The apostle Paul said in Philippians 4:11-13, "Not that I was ever in need, for I have learned how to be content with whatever I have. I know how to live on almost nothing or with everything. I have learned the secret of living in every situation, whether it is with a full stomach or empty, with plenty or little. For I can do everything through Christ who gives me strength." This is what we strive for. If we are blessed with material wealth we are content. This also means we don't feel guilty because we have it. We thank God everyday and do the wise and practical things we talked about above.

It's easy to drift back into basing security on worldly wealth – especially when we do have it. This is why it's so important to spend time becoming quiet and meditating on these truths. A good spiritual exercise is to check your heart and your willingness to give up all of your material possessions if God asked you to. Feel that resistance? It's okay, that's normal. The exercise is to quiet your mind and heart enough to get to a place inside where you truly are willing to let it all go. You begin to understand that no matter what, you'll be okay. This is true freedom. Again, it doesn't come naturally. Do it often.

People often misquote 1 Timothy 6:10 by saying that money is the root of all evil. This is not true. What the Scripture says is, "For the love of money is a root of all sorts of evil, and some by longing for it have wandered away from the faith and pierced themselves with many griefs." Again, the key word is love. It's also important to note Verse 9 prior to this says, "But those who want to get rich fall into temptation and a snare and many foolish and harmful desires which plunge men into ruin and destruction." The straightforward message here is, if we love money we will have pain and grief in our lives. It's a serious issue!

Wisdom is supernatural and that's why we need God to give it to us. A spiritual viewpoint of money doesn't come naturally and our inclination is to drift back to our old ways and attitudes about security … false security, that is. This is why it's important to spend time meditating on the truths in the Bible and checking our heart. The more we practice, the easier it is to live this new way of life. We develop a very low tolerance for the kind of pain described in 2 Timothy 6:9-10 above, and we quickly know where to go to get back to that sweet place of true security.

Proverbs 22 – HOW TO BE A GREAT EMPLOYEE

Read Proverbs 22.

There is great practical advice throughout Proverbs for workers. We all should be productive no matter what we do for a living - whether we work at home or outside the home. Whether we work for pay or volunteer our time, productivity and relationships with others is the key to success.

Verse 29 says, "Do you see any truly competent workers? They will serve kings rather than working for ordinary people." So, what does "truly competent" look like? We know the job we are assigned inside and out. We learn every skill necessary to be effective. We also make sure to address and manage every detail required to accomplish and complete the tasks required. For example, if you wait tables you learn the menu, the prices, and the procedures. If you're a new employee you ask questions until you know all you need to know.

Once we know our job inside and out, we learn and understand areas outside of our immediate responsibility. This same waitress could understand when food is delivered, and how the restaurant keeps track of inventory. Is the restaurant privately owned, or is it owned by a chain? What is the monthly revenue required to be profitable? These are some examples of looking outside your direct area of concern. Be wise in how you approach these questions, but most of all listen, observe, and learn.

We learn about the things that affect our work and how the output of our work affects others. Let's say we work as an accounts receivable clerk. In addition to knowing how we receive funds, we learn about the flow of information that comes into the department as well as the flow of information that goes out of the department along with other areas of the company. Some call it a "T" employee. The vertical bar of the T represents the deep knowledge you have within the function you work. The horizontal bar of the T represents your basic understanding of other parts of the organization. This will make you a better-rounded employee.

No matter what we do, we treat our jobs as if they are our business and we are the CEO.

The wise will go above and beyond in all these efforts. God wants us to shine, and He will give us what we need to do that.

We treat all individuals who we come in contact with, with respect. People are the most important thing to God, and He cares about how we interact with them. It's not always easy!

Some words of wisdom when it comes to dealing with people at work: don't take things personally and don't hold grudges. Honestly let go of any hurt feelings and, if you can, keep emotions to a minimum when it comes to work. Work is important, but it's just work. Have an emotional life outside of work with people you have intimate relationships with. Work is where you earn your living, it's not a place for drama. Fools create drama.

Sometimes in leadership positions in the workplace we must discipline and even fire people. This is for the good of the organization. Verse 10 says, "Throw out the mocker, and fighting goes too. Quarrels and insults will disappear." A constantly negative and complaining person in the workplace is awful. It's poison to the morale and adversely affects other workers. A good leader will see it and address it immediately for the good of the group.

Just as we see how poisonous a fool can be within an organization, we can also see how wisdom, respect, and graciousness affect environments in a positive way. If you respond to anger with respect and kindness, you'll see situations defuse. The Bible talks about this a lot.

In our homes we can't fire family members, but by raising kids in the way of wisdom, and providing a respectful example, they will model this behavior. As Verse 6 says, "direct your children on to the right path and when they are older, they will not leave it."

Ultimately, truly competent workers will be elevated and successful as we recall again from Verse 29. God will put us in positions we never dreamed possible, and He will give us the ability to be successful. Some days you may feel over your head, which is great! God wants us to stretch our abilities and to rely more fully on Him. On those days we pray Philippians 4:13 which reminds us, "I can do everything, through Christ who gives me strength."

If you feel unfulfilled in your work, then proactively take the steps to make changes. Go back to school, apply for a new job, or look for opportunities within your current job. If you are that waiter we talked about that is bored and frustrated, then do something about it. Sometimes it's simply a matter of changing our perspective. Maybe look at each table you serve as an opportunity to look into people's eyes or to memorize names. Start praying for God to open doors He wants open. We do the footwork and He will give us what we need.

If you actually hate your job, then chances are you are not being a good worker and it's time for a change. That is a miserable place to be! In the meantime, ask God to give you what you need and pray Philippians 4:13 as many times a day as you need to in order to stay focused and on-task. Also, thank God for the job you have, the income it provides, and the opportunity you've been given to grow. Very often we find that the jobs we couldn't stand are the ones that help us to appreciate every other job that comes after it. Endure for now and do the footwork to make a change.

Sometimes we need to quit a job before finding another one. This is a drastic measure and a lot of prayer, counsel from others, and wisdom should be pursued before taking this step. If you are convinced this is God's will, then step out and cling tightly and persistently to your faith.

God truly does want us to love our work. In fact, in seeking the meaning of all life, King Solomon came to this conclusion in Ecclesiastes 2:24, "So I decided there is nothing better than to enjoy food and drink and to find satisfaction in work. Then I realized that these pleasures are from the hand of God." In Ecclesiastes 3:13 he says, enjoying our work is a gift from God and in Verse 3:22 he says, there is nothing better for a person to do than to enjoy their work because that is their lot. So take heart if you are not happy at work, it is God's will that you enjoy your work, but He may have a reason for this season in your life. You will be blessed for being productive and faithful to Him.

If you have found yourself unemployed and are looking for work, now is the time to apply the wisdom we've talked about elsewhere in Proverbs. Trust God and don't allow fear a place in your heart or mind. This is easier said than done, but it is possible! In the meantime, you should still be productive. Your main job is to find a job, so do that work. Also, take the opportunity to get work done around your home and other areas where attention may be needed. It would be very good to volunteer to help others during this time. It will get you out of your own head and keep you occupied. Set your alarm to get up early every day and make a point not to waste time moping around or being lazy. Exercise. Read the Bible daily. It will make you feel better to be productive as you wait in faith for the next open door from God.

As long as we are allowing Him to guide all of our work, He will use us. That's the best work we can ever do.

Proverbs 23 – WHAT THE BIBLE SAYS ABOUT ALCOHOLISM

Read Proverbs 23.

In Alcoholics Anonymous they talk about how the only outcome to alcoholism is death or insanity. Verses 29 through 35 describe the miserable life of a person who abuses alcohol. The conclusion in Verse 35 perfectly describes the insanity AA talks about, "...when will I wake up so I can look for another drink?"

The life of a drunk is full of misery, anguish, sorrow, and conflict. Verse 29 asks who has unnecessary bruises and bloodshot eyes? Verse 34 describes the opposite of the stability and sanity we seek, "staggering like a sailor tossed at sea clinging to a swaying mast."

There is debate about what the Bible says about abstinence from alcohol. One thing is clear; abuse of alcohol is not associated with wisdom. In Ephesians 5:18 Paul says, "Don't be drunk with wine, because that will ruin your life. Instead, be filled with the Holy Spirit." This tells us that we cannot be intoxicated with mind or mood-altering chemicals and filled with the Holy Spirit at the same time. We seek to always be guided by God's sprit in order to live a life of wisdom, peace, and security.

Many wise people believe that it's better to abstain completely from alcohol since it really serves no good purpose. If you responded with the shrug of the shoulders and, "no big deal, I can take it or leave it," then you probably don't have a problem with addiction.

It can be difficult to self-diagnose whether or not there is a problem. Pray about it and ask for the truth to be revealed. Obviously if you have a life that is full of chaos, legal issues, or pain, due to booze then you need help. Oftentimes the evidence is more subtle and we can see it in our relationships with our loved ones. If drinking is causing a conflict with another person, then chances are it's a problem. If work or some other area of life is directly affected due to booze, then it may be time to look at it and nip it in the bud.

God has saved many people from the downward spiral of addiction. The first step is to admit there's a problem and ask Him for help. 12-step fellowships have meetings everywhere, all the time, and they are easy to access. They don't cost money and all are welcome. They are full of other people who can understand the struggles of alcoholism and they are great places to seek help. God is in these meetings if you look for Him and it may be where He wants to help you.

Others of us may not have the problem with alcohol, but love somebody who does. Loving a drunk or drug addict is arguably even more painful than being the substance abuser. It's best to not associate with alcoholics as Verse 20 says, but if it is a spouse or child you may have no choice. There is support through your church, the fellowship of Al-Anon, and other societal resources. The absolute most important first step is to let go and let God be in control. In these situations we find ourselves trying to control other people, and it's a miserable place to be. He loves the person more than you do and you have no control over others... believe it or not. You'll find immense freedom in letting go and trusting God. Remember Proverbs 3:5-6, "Trust in the Lord with all your heart; do not depend on your own understanding. Seek His will in all you do, and He will show you which path to take." Refer back to chapter 3 of this book if you need to. The dynamics of a relationship are altered when one person changes. You cannot change another person. You need to change. Only God can change you, and so you need to depend upon Him in this matter.

If there is an issue of safety, you must keep yourself and any children out of harm's way. Ask God to show the way and seek support through others. A large percentage of domestic abuse is alcohol related. If you are in a situation where there is abuse, you need to get help immediately. This will require courage and prayer on your part. If you belong to a church go to your pastor or a member of the church you trust. Hopefully by now you have a mentor you can reach out to. Oftentimes in these situations we've lived a life where we're hiding the truth from others because we are ashamed. It's time to break that lie.

Otherwise, if you have a choice, it's not wise to hang out with people who abuse alcohol or drugs. It will bring unnecessary drama into your life. If you are single and dating, it's definitely a red flag to watch out for.   It would be foolish to get deeply involved with someone who is a practicing alcoholic, or even possibly, someone who is a former alcoholic. You run the risk of this person relapsing. Keep your eyes wide open. For all practical purposes it's not something you want to invite into your life.   This is especially true if you have children.

If you have friends or relatives who have a problem, be honest as to why you are not going to associate with them. Maybe it's the wakeup call they need.   Needless to say, it's not your job to change them.   It's possible to love people without becoming emotionally enmeshed in their problems with alcohol or drugs. It should probably be at a distance whenever possible. If they truly want help, you still cannot change them, but you can direct them to the resources we've talked about and pray for them often. Then you let go and trust God.

Everyday wisdom is practical advice for life. Alcoholism and drug addiction extend beyond the purposes of this book.   That being said, we know God is very much involved and intimate with our lives. He is near and present, and He alone is the ultimate solution to all of our problems.   Seek Him with all your heart and you will find Him. In the meantime, do the footwork to get the help you need if you are in a situation where alcohol and drugs are destroying the life God intended for you to live. There is always hope.

Proverbs 24 – UNDERSTANDING SPIRITUAL WARFARE

Read Proverbs 24.

We would be fools to think we can live in this world and there would be no war. We are at war every day. Spiritual warfare is a battle that is real, and it takes place all around us everyday all the time.

Victory in war requires might. Proverbs 24:5 says "the wise are mightier than the strong, and those with knowledge grow stronger and stronger". In other words; strategy, planning, and contingencies trump brute force. Throughout our study of wisdom we've learned the importance of seeking the counsel of others. In fact, Verse 5 says victory depends on many advisors.

We are now applying wisdom to a very serious issue.

What is spiritual warfare? It is the battle between God and Satan for the hearts and minds of man. It is very real and crucial to understand this concept. In our everyday lives, it is in areas where we are tempted to choose the crooked paths such as lust, dishonesty, selfishness, or anger. We have a clear profile of what the crooked path looks like based on the conduct of the fool and the wicked throughout Proverbs.

We are on a quest for wisdom so we acknowledge there is a war being waged and we must have a good strategy. That strategy includes wise council from many advisers. In the book of Ephesians Verse 6:12, God lays out where the battle is; "For we do not wrestle against flesh and blood, but against the rulers, against the authorities, against the cosmic powers over this present darkness, against the spiritual forces of evil in the heavenly places." The evil and ugliness we see in this world is not about bad people. It's spiritual evil. When we struggle with anger with another person, or are tempted by foolish choices or opposition, it's a spiritual battle. We remind ourselves that our battle is not with flesh and blood.

When we are clear where the battlefield exists we are able to achieve victory in the war. We don't want to show up at the wrong location and fight the wrong enemy! Ephesians 6:13-17 provides further strategy for fighting this battle and how to arm ourselves. Interestingly, the only offensive weapon needed is contained in the 2nd part of Verse 17; the sword of the spirit which is the word of God.

When we study and absorb the Bible it becomes a powerful weapon in this war we are engaged in. Let's be clear, you are engaged whether you want to be or not. Hebrews 4:12 describes the Bible: "For the word of God is alive and powerful. It is sharper than the sharpest two-edged sword, cutting between soul and spirit, between joint and marrow." It's crucial that we create a lifelong habit of studying the Bible. It's the only way to grow in wisdom and to stand strong against the enemy.

Verse 15 in Ephesians 6 then gives us another powerful tool; prayer. When we pray the Word of God, we are tapping into power far greater than any evil that exists on earth. Jesus says in Matthew 18:20, "For where two or three are gathered in my name, there am I among them." In an extreme case of spiritual warfare, exorcism is real and it is scriptural. It always entails the Word of God and praying in the name of Jesus Christ to abolish demons.

Some excellent books that help portray spiritual warfare are fictional novels by Frank Peretti such as *This Present Darkness* and *Piercing the Darkness*. Although these are fictional novels, they portray spiritual warfare in a way that is tangible from the perspective of angels, demons, and humans. Peretti is a Christian author so his stories accurately depict that victory comes through the faithful prayers of believers and through the power of Scripture.

It's important not to glamorize spiritual warfare or demonic activity. It is real, but in the light of God's presence it has no power. We need to rest in the peace that comes from God and simply know that we have the power of victory through Him. Let there be no doubt about that! We have absolutely nothing to fear from evil.

We remember that fear of God is the beginning of knowledge and wisdom. When we refer back again to Proverbs 24: 5-6 where it says those with knowledge grow stronger and stronger, we see where our true strength lies. It lies in attaining wisdom through God. When we join with others in prayer as Verse 6 says, we have everything we need to be fierce warriors in this battle of life.

Proverbs 25 – A KEY TO MENTAL HEALTH

Read Proverbs 25.

Forgiveness is a vital key to mental health. Both receiving it and giving it. It's absolutely critical and necessary for spiritual health and it's the foundation of Christianity.

First, we must understand our desperate need for forgiveness, and the joy and peace that comes when we find it. Only then can true, deep-seated transformation take place. As usual, it starts with humility.

God knows every single thing about us, there is nothing hidden from Him. When we come to realize that He loves us anyway, it changes us. When we really, truly get what Jesus did on the cross, it should bring us to our knees in gratitude for God's plan of grace. The forgiveness of God brings a peace and self-acceptance that's impossible to have without this experience.

The grace and forgiveness of God is best characterized as a gift that is not deserved. Imagine someone giving you an amazing and precious gift for no reason whatsoever. In fact, maybe you've been rude to this person or treated them poorly. Then to receive this gift is the same concept of God's forgiveness. He doesn't have to forgive us. We certainly can't do anything that would make us worthy of this gift. The true gift is Jesus taking on the punishment for all of our crimes, sin, and ugliness, and paying the ultimate price. He didn't do it because He had to or because we are so worthy. He did it out of grace and mercy and, above all, love. As we've learned, God is a God of true justice. There needs to be payment for sin. Jesus did that for us.

It's a process. Every day we should search our hearts and ask God to forgive us as we strive to change and grow closer to Him. Chances are we'll spend our whole lives struggling with sin. A great thing to pray is in Psalm 139:23-24: "Search me, O God, and know my heart; Try me and know my anxious thoughts; and see if there be any hurtful way in me, And lead me in the everlasting way." It's a process of opening up every single place inside of our souls and willfully letting Him in to shine His light.

Many of us have dark and shameful places inside that we want to keep hidden. He doesn't force us to open those doors, but he waits patiently for us to let Him in to shine His light on the truth. That's when change starts to happen in our lives. If we confess our sins, he is faithful, and just to forgive us our sins and to cleanse us from all unrighteousness. (1 John 1:9)

Some of us have committed acts that are deeply shameful but have come to terms with the truth of our sin. Other times we cannot bear to face the truth and have justified our behaviors without facing them honestly. Abortion is one of those acts that many have experienced – both men and women. There are a lot of excuses and lies to justify abortion in our society. When we face the truth that we killed a baby and receive the loving forgiveness of God, only then can the healing process begin. We are comforted by the fact that those babies are in heaven. Sometimes we've abused others or have violated deeply-held moral principles. God knows them all; He loves you and is waiting to cleanse, heal and change you. It's not easy but it's simple and available to all.

A critical aspect of searching our heart is seeing where we are withholding forgiveness from others. Giving forgiveness to others is an ongoing process as we mature in our spiritual journey. It's also necessary in order to have peace in our hearts. If we truly understand our need for forgiveness, then we realize we have no right to withhold it from others.

In Matthew 18:26-32 Jesus tells the parable of the unforgiving servant. It's the story of a servant who, when he begged, was forgiven a huge debt by his master. Then this same forgiven slave turned around and demanded repayment by another who owed him money. In fact, he choked the guy and threw him in jail until he paid him back. It would be difficult to pay back debt in jail, so most likely the debt then fell on his family! In Verses 32-33 the original forgiving master heard about this and said, "You wicked slave, I forgave you all that debt because you pleaded with me. Should you not also have had mercy on your fellow slave, in the same way that I had mercy on you?" God is very serious about us forgiving others.

Those of us who have received the healing and peace that comes from forgiveness should really understand we have no right to withhold forgiveness from anybody else. A verse that is often misunderstood is Luke 6:37 where Jesus says, "Judge not, and you will not be judged; condemn not, and you will not be condemned; forgive, and you will be forgiven." This verse is not a blanket statement about not judging others, but actually about not being a hypocrite. For example, if you have struggled with sexual sin in your heart and have received forgiveness, you have no right to condemn another who is engaged in sexual sin. That being said, good judgment and discernment are part of a life of wisdom. Our judgment between right and wrong should align with what God believes is right and wrong. This becomes clearer as we continue to study His Word and seek His will. We start to hate what He hates and love what He loves. This does require judgment. It's just not our place to withhold forgiveness... He doesn't.

Forgiveness is definitely an emotional issue where we must deal with our resentments. It's also very much about actions. Verse 21 says if your enemies are hungry, give them food to eat, if they are thirsty, give them water to drink. Stop and think about someone you have resentment or a grudge toward. Now imagine showing that person kindness. The meaning of Verse 22 implies that the act will change that person and bring them to a place of repentance. If that's still too much for us yet, a good baby step is to sincerely pray for this

114

person every day for seven days. Sometimes it takes years to heal these resentments and to forgive. The important thing is to be willing.

The power of forgiveness and humility are supernaturally powerful and you never know what results will come. When we change it causes a ripple effect in the people around us. Verse 15 says patience can persuade a prince, and soft speech can break bones. This verse is a reflection of the power of a soft heart. Ultimately, forgiveness is a heart issue. Oftentimes, it's an ongoing process - especially when there is deep resentment and anger. Our actions help immensely in the process and they speak the loudest.

Shame and resentments are poisonous and evil, and are not from God. It's impossible to be at peace. People who receive God's forgiveness and willfully give forgiveness to others are mentally and emotionally healthy. They are living the benefits of a life of wisdom.

Proverbs 26 – HOW TO GROW SPIRITUALLY

Read Proverbs 26

If you've ever had a dog you've likely seen it eat its own vomit. It's disgusting! Verse 11 compares this to a fool who continues to repeat his foolishness. Insanity has been defined as repeating the same mistakes over and over but expecting different results. If we are trapped in a cycle of returning to the same sin over and over again, we understand the idea being conveyed here. It feels disgusting inside and consistently produces pain in our lives.

If we're being honest with ourselves and seeking God on a daily basis, persistent sin will become evident. As we mature in our spiritual walk, the deep-rooted sins become more subtle yet still troublesome. For example, we may have stopped stealing, lying, and cheating but can still recognize selfishness in our thinking. Maybe we have stopped a pattern of abusiveness, but acknowledge that we are still withholding forgiveness, or harboring resentment toward others.

It can be frustrating when we experience over and over again the cycle of sin/repent/sin/repent/sin/repent. It gets very old and causes discomfort in our heart in those quiet moments.

Guilt is not a bad thing. In fact, guilt is God prodding our hearts that there is something that He wants to change in us. There are those who would like to abolish guilt. You may have seen the bumper sticker "screw guilt." That's not wisdom. For example, we may look back on our day and feel guilty for not spending enough time with our kids. Why is that guilt a bad thing? Guilt is something we should definitely be sensitive to and immediately address with God. It's time to make a change. Shame is different. Shame is not from God. Shame is telling you that you are rotten, and worthless, and will never change. Shame tells us that we aren't good enough for God to love us. Don't let unaddressed guilt turn to shame. Consider guilt a call to change. Consider shame vomit and a lie.

If you are struggling with shame that is causing destruction in your life, seek help from a strong Christian mentor. Most of all, seek God. He loves and adores you. He is the only one who can truly heal shame. This is specifically why He sent His son Jesus. He came to heal us. He can and will heal you.

The most important thing is to spend quiet, intimate time with God everyday and purposely let Him in. We let Him show us where we are going sideways. This isn't about condemnation; it's about letting Him change us. Psalm 139:23-24 says, "Search me, O God, and know my heart; Try me and know my anxious thoughts; And see if there be any hurtful way in me, And lead me in the everlasting way." (NIV) These verses describe a loving and trusting relationship with a God who adores us. The previous verses in Psalm 139 reflect the passion and obsession that He has for us. Check them out.

There are character flaws in us that we have tried and tried to change but continue to cave in to the temptation and act in ways we hate. It feels like returning to cold vomit. There are some things that we just can't change about ourselves; otherwise we would have done it a long time ago! You can't fix a broken tool with a broken tool. This is where the miracles happen. God will change us if we let Him.

We realize our spiritual journey is a lifelong striving toward improvement and growth. The Bible says no one is righteous. (Romans 3:10) Not Mother Theresa, not your pastor, not Billy Graham. No one is perfectly holy...except God. We should feel very secure that we have a perfect God – there is no sin or darkness in Him. In a world where moral standards are fluid and questionable, we have a rock to stand upon.

You can be assured if you've reached this phase of your walk, you have been changed and transformed, and God will continue to make changes in you. Hopefully, you have experienced the freedom that comes with knowing God adores you just as you are, right where you're at. Ironically, when we realize we can never earn God's love by "being good enough", we are free to accept His unconditional love. There is no longer condemnation and we are free to finally grow. Surely He is delighted with the progress you've made.

Think back to when you first started this journey in your relationship with God. The person you were then – your thoughts, motives, and behaviors – have changed. For a lot of us the change is drastic. If you're just starting out on this journey on the knowledge of God, then you should be seeing obvious changes in yourself. Wisdom has been said to be God's perspective. Your perspective has changed as you allow His wisdom to transform you.

The road really does become more narrow…yet we are more free.

There is something miraculous that happens inside of us when we allow the Word of God to penetrate our hearts and minds. Romans 12:2 says, "Do not be conformed to this world, but be transformed by the renewal of your mind, that by testing you may discern what is the will of God, what is good and acceptable and perfect." Our mind is supernaturally renewed when we study the Bible. Our tolerance for the pain that sin causes gets lower and lower as we continue to grow in wisdom and our lives are healed. We stop returning to the cold, nasty vomit of foolishness.

None of us will ever behave perfectly, but we can continue to make forward progress in our spiritual walk. The way we continue forward is to nurture our relationship with God through daily prayer and Bible study. It's not about trying harder but surrendering everything to Him. It's actually pretty simple! He changes us from the inside out. We start to love what He loves and hate what He hates. Going backward is no longer an option that makes any sense.

Proverbs 27 – MARRIAGE ADVICE

Read Proverbs 27.

Throughout Proverbs you see verses where it talks about a nagging or quarrelsome wife as in Verse 15: "A quarrelsome wife is as annoying as constant dripping on a rainy day." Back in Proverbs 26:24 it says it's better to live alone in an attic than in a beautiful home with a nagging wife.

Marriage is difficult and even the best of them require work. Marriage was created by God to be between a man and woman from the very beginning of creation. He made woman from man's flesh (Genesis 2:22). In Genesis 2:23 the man's first response was, "At last!" "For this reason a man shall leave his father and his mother, and be joined to his wife; and they shall become one flesh. And the man and his wife were both naked and were not ashamed" Genesis 2:23-24. It's very good and it is a sacred institution ordained by God.

The reality in our world today is divorce rates are depressingly high. This includes within the Christian church. This is not God's plan. Many of us have experienced the pain and consequence of divorce. Yet, also for most of us, there is the natural instinct to bond with a lifelong mate. This is normal and healthy and the way God designed us.

If you are remarried after divorce, the bottom line scriptural truth we must cling to is that our God is a God of second, third, and

120

endless chances. We also know He is a healer and our marriage can bring healing where once there was brokenness.

If we are married we need to be committed to staying married, and be willing to do the work to keep our marriages healthy. Pray for your marriage every day. Ask God to change what needs to be changed in you in order to stay married the rest of your life.

If we are single, we need to ensure that we make good choices going forward and let God direct our decisions and make the needed changes inside us. Pray every day for wisdom and protection from wrong choices in a mate. This is a huge topic for another time. For now, we'll focus on good marriage advice from the One who created marriage.

In Ephesians 5:33 God in His wisdom gives foundational marriage counsel. He tells women to respect their husbands and a husband to love his wife. Women are to look up to their husbands as the leader, and men are to cherish and put their wives before themselves. Both are to serve the other. The irony of this is that these are things that do not come naturally for men and women.

Women have a tendency to criticize, control, and want to change their husbands. This is not respectful. On the other hand, to love, cherish, and nurture does not usually come naturally for men. They typically keep feelings inside and often have a hard time responding to a woman's emotions. At its worst, in a marriage, you have a woman who is hypercritical, nagging, and constantly putting down her husband. At the same time you may have a husband who is completely shut down emotionally, cold, self-centered, and detached from his wife. The walls of resentment are a mile high. It's safe to say in this scenario the sex life is non-existent or even a painful aspect of the relationship. Both are miserable. This isn't God's plan.

A man thrives on his woman's respect and can instantly be lifted up when his wife praises him (especially in public), and when she accepts him for who he is. He is confident in the love of his wife. A woman who is loved, cherished, and adored by her husband has a special and beautiful glow that transcends physical beauty. She is confident in the love of her husband. Affection, loving words, acts of helping, a small gift, or a romantic date at a coffee shop can demonstrate your love for her.

Why would God wire us in ways where His vision of marriage is not natural for us? Maybe it's so we would depend upon Him throughout our life and marriage. Marriage is hard work and it requires both parties to be humble. As we are learning in a life of wisdom, it's about taking the right action. Usually it starts with the way we think.

If you're married, try the following experiments: First, ask God to direct your thoughts toward your spouse.

Wives, create a story in your mind where your husband is a hero. You know him. You know in what kind of situation he would be a hero. Maybe it's coming across a lost child or a sick animal.

Maybe it's a situation where he would protect you from zombies. Spend time with this little fantasy and play it out in your mind. That's all. Then see if your attitude toward him changes a little bit.

Husbands, listen to music and when a love song comes on where a man is singing to a woman imagine singing that song to your wife. Say crazy, over-the-top loving words out loud to yourself about your adoration for her when you're alone in your car. You know her and the things that make her special. This is just you practicing to see how it feels inside. No pressure. You may not have the guts (or the voice) to actually say those words or sing that song. That's okay for now, we're taking baby steps. See if it changes your perspective of your wife.

Even if you don't feel it, show your spouse some love. Verse 5 says, "an open rebuke is better than hidden love!" Withholding love is another response to hurt and resentment. What we're doing is more important than what we're feeling. Hard hearts destroy marriages. These acts will soften hearts.

God adores your mate and accepts him/her for exactly who they are. He created them as unique individuals exactly the way He wanted. Make the effort to count up the good qualities of your spouse. Take the time to look them in the eyes and give them a genuine smile.

Finally, forgiveness is the other necessity for a strong marriage. This reflects the heart of God and is something on which we must place the highest value.

With God, it always boils down to humility and subservience. These are not qualities that are "normal" in our world, and this is why we need Him. With God's strength, we are able to do and be far more than we ever could without Him. This includes having a healthy marriage and living a life of wisdom.

Proverbs 28 – ANOTHER KEY TO MENTAL HEALTH

Read Proverbs 28

There is a saying among the people of the Catholic religion that they don't need psychiatrists because they go to confession. In their religious practice they go to a priest to confess their sins in complete confidentiality. Assumedly this means they can confess every single thing that they have ever done or thought. There is actually a lot of wisdom in this.

Proverbs 28:13 tells us that people who conceal their sins will not prosper, but if they confess and turn from them they will receive mercy.

There is a saying you often hear in the 12-step fellowships that "we are as sick as our secrets." James 5:16 says to confess your sins to each other and pray for each other so that you may be healed.

We know that nothing is hidden from God. There are no secrets from him and he knows every deed and thought. In His love for us and in His wisdom, He tells us to tell another person all of our secrets. This may be terrifying for some of us and we immediately balk at the idea.

Maybe we've committed crimes or even atrocities in our past that could have severe consequences if admitted. Maybe we are deeply ashamed and feel we could never tell another person things we've vowed not to reveal. We don't want to think about these buried secrets ever again. Maybe we're just too embarrassed. We just want to put that stuff behind us.

Some of us may be wrestling with some persistent sin in our life that is making us feel bad. We can't seem to get out of the rut of sin/repent/sin/repent. Yet, we put a lot of effort into maintaining a shiny image on the outside. We have put ourselves on a pedestal of perfection and can't let others know we struggle. It gets to a point where it would be completely humiliating to reveal the truth.

These secrets are poison to our soul. They feed the ugly lies of shame that stop our spiritual growth. They prevent us from being mentally and emotionally healthy. This is worth repeating; people who harbor secrets can never be emotionally healthy. It's time to trust wisdom and bring the secrets out into the light. It's time for freedom.

Open your heart to God first. By now this should be pretty easy. Become quiet and face Him with all these things you unconsciously (or consciously) have hidden deep in your heart. Ask him to forgive you and then accept His forgiveness. Remember 1 John 1:9 says, "But if we confess our sins to him, he is faithful and just to forgive us our sins and to cleanse us from all wickedness." It actually helps to do this on our knees.

If you have a shameful secret where you may have been a victim, ask Him to heal you and ask Him to forgive the other person.

The hatred and resentment you may feel is also poisonous to your soul. There is a lot of power in asking God to forgive that person, even if you aren't yet able to. The important thing right now is to get it out of the darkness and into the light.

Do some writing.

Whatever your secrets are, willingly go to your loving Father and let Him in to every space inside. Next, ask Him to give you wisdom to find the right, trustworthy, and wise people to talk to. Maybe it's a pastor, a close friend, a spouse, a counselor, or even a Catholic priest. Ask God to give you the courage to say it out loud.

When you finally have this crucial conversation, ask this person to pray with you and for you. This is not easy but it's necessary.

If we do these things, we will experience a supernatural healing and lightness in our soul. There is a reason it is wise to confess out loud. If you are in the cycle of sin/repent/sin/repent change the pattern to sin/repent/confess.

Find an accountability partner. Seek someone who is of the same sex and who is on the same page spiritually. Commit to meeting together regularly. Ask about each other's prayer life and thought life. Hold each other accountable and be trustworthy to listen to their confessions in complete confidentiality. Vow to faithfully keep each other's confidences.

If you belong to a church, take the opportunity to join small groups – sometimes called "life groups." This is the place where you develop intimate relationships and build the trust to grow in this way. If you belong to a church and are not part of a small group, you need to join one.

If you truly desire wisdom but don't belong to a church you should honestly consider it. Usually local community churches are great options. A thriving and alive church will offer smaller more intimate groups to grow together in study of the Bible. If you've had bad experiences with church, you should be grateful in the knowledge that most of us have a lot of different options to find a church that is a good fit. The reason why this is important is this is where you can build relationships like we've been talking about. It's time to commit.

God wants us to experience this life with other people. He knows how He made us. God is all about intimate relationships. We can't get away with staying shallow when it comes to the life God wants for us. He is passionate about our relationship with Him, and our relationship with others.

This then should become a regular practice for us; search our hearts for sin, ask God to forgive and change us, confess out loud to another person whenever necessary, and don't allow any secrets to fester. We are being changed from the inside out.

Proverbs 29 – RAISING CHILDREN

Read Proverbs 29.

Raising kids is one of the most difficult and most important things we do in life. It's something that God talks a lot about in the Bible and in Proverbs. Proverbs 22:6 says, "Train up a child in the way he should go, even when he is old he will not depart from it." (NASB)

Discipline your kids. This basic wisdom, when followed, bears good fruit in our lives, our kid's lives, and in society. As with most wisdom, it's simple but it's not always easy.

In today's culture, the disintegration of the family has added a layer of difficulty and pain to raising kids. There are families that are split up and trying to blend with other families, there are single parents and grandparents all trying to raise kids. There are even kids raising kids.

The most heartbreaking aspect of divorce is the impact it has on children. This is not to cast shame on divorced parents. Many of us have gone through divorce and probably all of us have been affected by divorce. We must face the truth if we are to employ wisdom in our lives.

Once divorced, the parents are able to move on with their lives. Kids have to go through the rest of their childhood experiencing heartbreak every other weekend. They have to deal with missing one of the parents all the time. It's almost always confusing and painful for them no matter the age. Divorce damages kids. That's the truth and it hurts! There are a lot of different circumstances around every situation but the suffering of the kids is a common denominator. That means we must be extra vigilant when it comes to trying to raise kids right. Thankfully we have a God of compassion, healing, and wisdom to guide us through His Word in all situations.

Within one generation our culture has made drastic changes. No longer does divorce carry the stigma it used to. In the past couples used to "stay married for the kids." Based on today's divorce rates, that's no longer as common. Obviously, it's much better for kids to be in a family that is cemented together by a happy marriage.

Many kids are born into single-parent homes. In these cases, we need to keep our kids safe and make wise choices when it comes to dating and the people we bring into their lives. We also need to accept that we can't do everything. Do what you can and then rely on other family members or safe people in your life. Ideally, there are members of the opposite sex who can help support you and your kids emotionally while you're single. Kids need both a male and female influence whenever possible. Again, the most important thing is that they are kept safe.

Any of us who have been in a single-parent situation knows the longing that comes when we see a family together. We don't know if they're happy or not, but in our minds they have something we don't.

Don't let this longing cause you to turn in desperation to the first person who comes along. Too many times this ends up in disaster. It's vitally important that we try to let God fulfill our emotional and intimacy needs. Fall in love with the Lord. It's not easy – we have flesh that is strong and causes us to make foolish choices.

These situations can make disciplining our kids more complicated. If divorced, we feel guilty because we know they've been hurt. We may not see them all the time so we don't want our limited time together to be spent disciplining them. Maybe you are a grandparent and are just too darn tired! Even a two-parent traditional family can struggle with disciplining children.

Whatever our situation, it's important for us to understand that disciplining our kids is good for them. Repeat: it is good for them. It makes them feel secure when there are boundaries and limitations. They need to be supervised and given good direction while they're in our care. There needs to be consequences to wrong actions, no matter what age, and the earlier we start the better.

Spanking kids is a good thing according to the Bible. Refer to Proverbs 13:24 and Proverbs 23:13. It's a useful disciplinary tool up to around the age of ten years old. They need to understand that when they do something wrong there are painful consequences that hurt. It helps them to grow up to be stable, healthy adults.

When spankings are done in a loving way, and that doesn't mean softly, the kid feels better! Seriously. A plan should be established in advance between the parents regarding spankings. It's always good to communicate ahead of time so you're on the same page before the situation comes up.

The right way to spank a kid is not out of anger or reactionary. If you are angry put them in a time-out before taking action. When you're ready, sit them down and explain that they are getting a spanking. Make sure they understand why they are being punished. Then spank there little butts hard enough to hurt. Afterwards leave them alone to think about it. This is probably the hardest part. After a period of time go to them and have them tell you why they got spanked. This reinforces the fact that they are suffering from consequences of their own actions. It's not because you're mean. This helps prevent them from playing the victim and enforces the concept of personal responsibility. Some good words to say are, "I know you did a bad thing but I also know you are a good boy. I love you very much." Then hold their face in your hands and give them a big smooch and hug them. This is by far the best part. Do not apologize for spanking them.

This might sound mean, but they should cry. They should feel bad for being bad. Think about it, we only get saved through repentance. Our kids need to understand what repentance feels like. Of course, we follow on with the model of our Lord and we love them unconditionally as well. They know we forgive them when they're sorry. Our kids feel safe and secure in our love.

Shortly after this type of discipline, you will likely see a child who feels happy and content and it shows. Even better, you'll be working toward a child who has a change in behavior. These are basic tactics that are well known by parents who believe in disciplining their kids. They also get to enjoy the positive results of well-disciplined children. You probably enjoy being around those kids yourself.

As Verse 17 says, discipline your children, and they will give you peace; they will bring you the delights you desire. We are passing wisdom along to our children through strong boundaries. This is in contrast to Verse 15 where it describes a child left undisciplined disgraces its mother. Being around well-behaved children is wonderful and enjoyable. Kids who are out of control are extremely disruptive and irritating. Bratty kids are unlikeable and it's not their fault. We've all been around them. The parents are to blame, but the kids take the brunt.

As kids get older other methods are more effective such as taking away privileges. The challenge is to have clear boundaries and rules, stay consistent, and stick to your guns. It will pay off.

We have a responsibility to discipline our kids no matter their age or the situation in which we are raising them. Nobody does it perfectly, it is definitely not easy, and we will most likely mess it up. That doesn't mean we stop trying! The good news is, we don't have to be perfect, we just have to make the effort and trust God to fill in the gaps. We will see the benefits when we follow the path of wisdom in this matter.

Proverbs 30 - WHAT IS TRUTH?

Read Proverbs 30.

If something is right for you, depending on your circumstances, then it's right. It may not be right for me but it is for you. If something is wrong for you but not me, then that's your truth but not mine. Stop and think about those statements. How does it make you feel? We might feel a moment of relief. If we are trying to justify some behavior in our lives, we might want to agree with these concepts. The basis of this philosophy is that there is no real truth. Pontius Pilate said sarcastically to Jesus, just before he turned Him over to be crucified, "What is truth?" (John 18:38) This is called moral relativism and it is not God's way. It's not wisdom.

Moral relativism is like the verses in Matthew 7:24-27 where Jesus talks about building a house on shifting sand instead of building on a solid foundation of rock. A house built on an unstable foundation is unsound and will collapse in a storm. We want to build our house on the solid foundation of the truth where our house stands strong through any storm of life.

Examples of convenient morality are highlighted in this chapter of Proverbs. Verse 12 says, "they are pure in their own eyes, but they are filthy and unwashed." Along the same lines Verse 20 says, "an adulterous woman consumes a man, then wipes her mouth and says,

135

'What's wrong with that?'" When there is no standard it's easy to justify any type of behavior or lifestyle.

By now, we've been able to experience the healing, cleansing, and security that comes with following God's path of wisdom. It has changed us from the inside out. God is the author of truth. There is no gray area. Right is right and wrong is wrong. There is a lot of power in understanding that His truth is inside of us. We also have the power to defeat any temptation. In John 14:6 Jesus said of Himself that; He is the way, the truth, and the life. Either it's true or it's not. What do you believe?

We know in our conscience what is right and if we need guidance we have his Word, the Bible. He will always show us the right path in life if we let Him.

Verse 5 says, "Every word of God proves true. He is a shield to all who come to him for protection." 2 Timothy 3:16 states, "All Scripture is inspired by God and is useful to teach us what is true and to make us realize what is wrong in our lives. It corrects us when we are wrong and teaches us to do what is right." All Scripture is inspired by God and the entire Bible is true. All of it.

Now is the time to commit to reading the Bible. An excellent way to get a good start is to get a *New Living Translation Study Bible*. New Living Translation reads as a very modern translation and is easy to relate to. No matter what translation, a study bible is essential. It provides insight and teachings about the various Scriptures by Bible scholars. If you were learning a new skill, you would naturally seek knowledge from the experts. A study Bible provides insight, commentary, and articles by those experts. It makes for a fascinating and enjoyable read.

Okay, some people hate to read, (they're probably not reading this book). That's no excuse. There are audible Bible apps you can download, books on audio, and sermons on the radio.

However you do it, you must continue to feed or you'll starve. The proven ideal is to study the Scripture and spend regular quiet time with God. He can only speak to us when we are quiet, and He speaks to us through His word - loud and clear.

A good place to start if you are new to Bible study is in the Book of John, Psalms, and Proverbs. There are fascinating stories and incredible adventures in the Old Testament. The Bible is the most interesting historical book you will ever read.

Acquiring wisdom is an ongoing, lifelong mission. It should be enjoyable and enriching as well. According to Hebrews 4:12, "For the word of God is living and active." You can read the Bible cover to cover 100 times and it will continue to provide new and fresh insight. A life of wisdom requires that you be in the Word on a regular basis.

We need a moral compass in life that provides a "true north." A compass that changes with the wind just leaves us stranded and lost. In the Old Testament, God created the Ten Commandments (Exodus 20:1-17) to give His people basic rules for right and wrong. In the

New Testament, Jesus expanded on those laws to address motives of the heart. In Matthew 5:27-28 he says, "You have heard that it was said, you shall not commit adultery; but I say to you that everyone who looks at a woman with lust for her has already committed adultery with her in his heart." It's not just about doing right on the outside, but making sure our hearts are right.

As we grow in wisdom we grow in discernment. In the dictionary discernment is defined as, the ability to see and understand people, things, or situations clearly and intelligently (Merriam Webster). More specifically, biblical discernment can be described as the ability to think biblically. We are able to recognize the lies of moral relativism and false wisdom when we know the real truth. False teaching will not sit right in your gut.

God knows a solid foundation of morality is what we need to live a life that is full of joy, peace, and security. He is our rock.

Proverbs 31- STRIVING FOR PERFECTION

Read Proverbs 31.

Proverbs 31 wraps up the Book of Proverbs with the description of the perfect woman. Don't let this depress you; it's an excellent ideal to strive for. It perfectly sums up Proverbs with a picture of a life lived in wisdom. It should give us hope!

Verses 10-31 describe a marriage where the husband completely trusts his wife and she makes him proud. The life of a highly productive person is portrayed here. This is a person who makes wise financial decisions and is an excellent provider for the family. Exceptional business sense and a loving, stable family are kept in balance. Her children are well-behaved and respectful toward her and she is praised greatly by her husband.

Proverbs 31:17 even touches on physical fitness: "She dresses herself in strength and makes her arms strong." It's safe to assume God made our bodies to be active. In today's society we need to put in the effort to remain physically fit.

Back in Proverbs 1:2-4 we recall the foundational purpose of Proverbs; "Their purpose is to teach people wisdom and discipline, to help them understand the insights of the wise. Their purpose is to teach people to live disciplined and successful lives, to help them do what is right, just, and fair. These proverbs will give insight to the simple, knowledge and discernment to the young." The person described in Proverbs 31 has embraced this purpose and is living a life of wisdom.

We also remember the key point back in Proverbs 1:7 that fear of the Lord is the foundation of true knowledge. In Proverbs 31:25 it perfectly reflects the deep security we experience when we've acquired this wisdom; "She is clothed with strength and dignity, and she laughs without fear of the future." There is nothing that can shake a life that is built on the rock solid foundation of God's wisdom. This security is not dependent upon our outside circumstances. That being said, by walking with integrity and strength, our lives produce good results. We set ourselves up for success by conducting ourselves in ways that are above reproach. When we are at peace with God and with others, we don't invite unnecessary trauma and destruction into our lives.

Growing in wisdom is an ongoing process for the rest of our days on this Earth. In Philippians 3:12 the Apostle Paul says, "I don't mean to say that I have already achieved these things or that I have already reached perfection. But I press on to possess that perfection for which Christ Jesus first possessed me." We continue to strive for that perfection. Don't take this as a point of shame or the burden of never being good enough. Only God is perfect all the time. We strive toward God and let Him be the ideal standard we strive for. The combination of His perfection and His grace takes away any feelings of inadequacy because we know He loves us no matter what. His love is perfect and unconditional. His perfection also includes forgiveness.

God's love doesn't change when we don't act or think right. He loved us long before we ever turned to Him. He wants to make our lives better and He knows best what we need. He created us.

People will notice something about you. The very last verse in the Book of Proverbs says to let her deeds be publicly praised. When you're changed from the inside out, the results will show on the outside. It's called fruit. In Matthew 7:20 Jesus said, "Yes, just as you can identify a tree by its fruit, so you can identify people by their actions." This provides an opportunity to bring others with us on the path of wisdom and as Verse 26 says, "when she speaks her words are wise, and she gives instructions with kindness." When you have Scripture buried in your mind you are able to give wise, biblical counsel. It pierces the heart - just as your heart has been pierced.

You have a foundation that is unshakeable, and a relationship with a God who is unchanging. Meanwhile, you are constantly changing and growing as you continue to seek wisdom. You have gained tools for everyday living, and enjoy the blessing of true security. Let fear have no place in your life, and have reverence for God. Serve others. It doesn't get much better than that!

Thank you for reading my book. I hope you were able to draw closer to the Lord and have cultivated a new and growing passion for the wisdom in His precious Word and have realized the life-changing power within the scripture. I also hope this book proves to be a resource for you time and time again as you navigate this life.

If you enjoyed this book, won't you please take a moment to leave me a review at Amazon, Goodreads or your favorite ebook retailer. Your input is welcomed and valuable.

God bless!

Cynthia Down

Also available in ebook and paperback: Everyday Wisdom For Leaders by Cynthia Down

ABOUT THE AUTHOR

Cynthia is not your average "perfect" Christian, although she's sure they're out there somewhere! It's safe to say plenty of wild oats have been sown along the way. She has been an unmarried mom, a single mom, a boss, a member of the 12-step fellowships, a wife and an ex-wife, has had an abortion, and has suffered misery from a life focused on self.

Serious commitment to being in The Word on a regular basis for the past thirteen years has changed her life from the inside out. She is passionate about the transformative power of Scripture, and provides compelling biblical instruction and insight. She has been trained in leadership and biblical counsel through Healing Hearts Ministries International. She has a special place in her heart for post-abortive women.

Her mission is to provide everyday wisdom and advice that is completely relevant to today's culture, and is one hundred percent based on sound biblical truth. Her desire is that others will experience the unshakeable security that can only come through a deeper knowledge of God.

She'll openly share life and lessons with you through her blog, social media, and Everyday Wisdom books. You can contact her at:

Facebook: Everyday Wisdom

Twitter: @everdaywisdom77

Website: www.everydaywisdom.life

www.ingramcontent.com/pod-product-compliance
Lightning Source LLC
Chambersburg PA
CBHW070633030426
42337CB00020B/3997